The Making of the 20th Century

This series of specially commissioned titles focuses attention on significant and of often controversial events and themes of world history in the present century. Each book provides sufficient narrative and explanation for the newcomer to the subject while offering, for more advanced study, detailed source-references and bibliographies, together with interpretation and reassessment in the light of recent scholarship.

In the choice of subjects there is a balance between breadth in some spheres and detail in others; between the essentially political and matters economic or social. The series cannot be a comprehensive account of everything that has happened in the twentieth century, but it provides a guide to recent research and explains something of the times of extraordinary change and complexity in which we live. It is directed in the main to students of contemporary history and international relations, but includes titles which are of direct relevance to courses in economics, sociology, politics and geography.

The Making of the 20th Century

Series Editor: GEOFFREY WARNER

Further titles are in preparation

France and Decolonisation
1900–1960

Raymond F. Betts

St. Martin's Press   New York

First published in the United States of America in 1991

Printed in Hong Kong

ISBN 0-312-06050-5

Library of Congress Cataloging-in-Publication Data
Betts, Raymond F.
France and decolonisation 1900–1960 / Raymond F. Betts
p.   cm.—(The Making of the 20th century)
Includes bibliographical references and index.
ISBN 0-312-06050-5
1. Decolonization—France—History—20th century. 2. France—
Colonies—Administration—History—20th century. I. Title.
II. Series.
JV1818.B48   1991
325'.3144'0904—dc20   90–22403
                                                            CIP

Contents

Preface

This study is designed to analyse those twentieth-century activities that comprise colonial rule and colonial opposition, as well as those values and institutions which provided structure and purpose for both. However disparate in origin, setting and expression these cultural elements may seem, they have conveniently been gathered together under the overarching term 'decolonization', a term that suggests a process, if not a predetermined condition, that was first pronounced after World War II.

Spread around the world and across several decades, the changes that led to the end of the French colonial empire are a complicated part of a major shift in contemporary world affairs. That history, already debated acrimoniously and analysed carefully, merits being reviewed yet another time, 30 years after the last of the major colonial possessions gained their independence from France.

As an introductory history, the text that follows considers the course of empire, not as if projected on a mercator map, but topically, according to major issues and formative events. As with any work of synthesis, this one relies not only on the many scholarly monographs that have examined particular problems of French colonialism but also on preceding works which have examined broader issues and larger segments of France Overseas, as the collection of territories was once proudly described.

My own scholarly interest in the French colonial empire has been a long professional one, enriched by research in many libraries and archives, enlivened by visits to many of the places that once were part of that empire. Therefore, I acknowledge the beneficial cultural opportunities I have had to visit Algeria and Tahiti as well as the scholarly opportunities I have had to study and do research in Paris and Dakar. While I need thank no one individual for assistance in the writing of this brief text, I do gladly acknowledge a lifelong accumulation of indebtedness to the many who have assisted me, encouraged me and who have had the patience to criticise my previous work on this subject, work which provides the unseen foundation of this volume.

As I have done many times before with delight, I now do again: I express my deep appreciation for the strong support of my wife, Jackie, who has also kindly served as copy editor of this text and, before that, as counsellor urging on the completion of the book.

Many years ago, when I first travelled to West Africa, I found myself walking alone along a dirt road which was some distance north of Abidjan in the Ivory Coast. It was a hot day. An African suddenly emerged from the bush; he was carrying a machete and a bunch of palm fronds. I was carrying a camera. We approached; he smiled and then remarked in French, 'It certainly is hot, isn't it?' 'Yes, indeed,' I replied and smiled in return. We each continued along our individual ways.

Here was what sociologists would call an example of 'culture contact', one with little general significance, but of sufficient personal note to have caused me to wonder then, when it occurred, and to cause me to wonder still, as I now think back on it, what does it all mean, that French colonial experience, now that it has been silently transferred to the files of the archives and quietly reassessed on the pages of the history text?

RAYMOND F. BETTS

To the memory of Ambroise Jobert, teacher and friend, *grenoblois* whose vision extended far beyond his particular place.

Introduction: The French Colonial Empire in the Context of Modern History

There was no poet in France who celebrated empire, the excitement it engendered and the dismay it caused, as did Rudyard Kipling who regarded those lands over which the Union Jack waved. This particular lack of expression should not be surprising, any more than should the general lack of interest, scholarly as well as popular, in the history of that French colonial empire which occupied territory of considerable proportions in the early twentieth century, even if its physical size was not matched by its political weight in the balance of international affairs. In many ways, all nineteenth-century national expressions of imperialism were made on the edge of activities deemed most important and imperative. Unlike the most striking examples of twentieth-century imperialism, which are those of Nazi Germany, Imperial Japan and the Soviet Union, the colonial expansion of France did not arouse global interest, nor was its impact very noticeable in the daily life of the city dweller in Paris or Timbutoo, the peasant of Provence or the Mekong Delta. Even among its more closely engaged participants, the situation did not often lend much truth to the title of Bronislaw Malinowski's famous book, *The Dynamics of Culture Contact* (1945). Aside from one or two rather bustling cities in the early twentieth century, Saigon and Casablanca immediately come to mind, the social activities and the personal engagement in the French colonial empire were generally uninspiring and uneventful. The comments of L. Canard, commandant of the area of Dakar, Senegal, in the late nineteenth century, are worth noting. In his report of May 1877, he wrote: 'No commerce, no industry, no new inhabitants'. Then, in April 1879, he commented: 'The numerous ships in our harbor give a little life to our pseudo-city of Dakar, but commerce is as usual of a hopeless nullity, absolutely nothing but waffle-vendors'.[1]

Grand in the rhetoric which supported it, French imperialism was actually expressed in a series of small actions, involving relatively

1

few people. The big moments, and the agonising ones, occurred when the resulting empire was pulled apart, when the dreadfully long, terrible wars of national liberation in Vietnam and Algeria occurred. Seen at a distance and in such broad outline, the history of the French colonial empire reveals its asymmetrical shape: its relatively uneventful beginnings and its most eventful endings.

Among the prevailing theories that attempt to explain imperialism as a multi-national, globally-extensive phenomenon, there are those which suggest that such expansion was possible only because of the general indifference of the home population and because of the political disarray in those regions which did become colonial. Thus, the enterprise was perceived to be 'empire on the cheap', initially costly to no Frenchman and immediately of little consequence to most of those who were now supposedly in the shade provided by the French tricolour.

The prevailing metaphors which were and still are used to explain the cultural geography of imperialism are 'core' and 'periphery', terms that contrive a global geometry of concentric circles in which the innermost is the most significant. Put otherwise, the focus and the locus of modern European history was the nation state on the Continent. Thus Chancellor Otto von Bismarck once remarked 'My map of Africa lies in Europe'. While there is no French political figure of the time who was given to constructing epigrams as memorable as were Bismarck's, the French generally entertained similar sentiments about that disarray of territories called *France d'Outre-Mer*, Overseas France.

Acquired by few, enthusiastically received by a few more, disparaged by some and ignored by most, the French colonial empire was nevertheless an important fact or, better, a series of facts in modern history, particularly if the geometry of geography just referred to is replaced by a cultural algebra in which the factors are seen as having been variable and in which the expressions were frequently altered, while the principal equation was one concerned with political and social relationships. Thus plotted or described, European imperialism was disruptive and disturbing, but also innovative. Imperialism was an 'agent of modernization', the particular means by which railroads, double-entry bookkeeping, wage labour, innoculations and khaki shorts were introduced to other parts of the world which had been previously without them. But the French effort was also distinctive, as is evidenced in one minor development: the extensive use of the handshake as a means of greeting.

The historical encounter of peoples from different environments – perhaps 'ecologies' is a better word – suggests that the history of French decolonisation must go beyond the political facts of the matter to those conditions encapsulated in the terms 'culture contact' and 'colonial situation', to that complicated encounter which engendered curiosity and suspicion, respect and contempt, hope for reform and desire for revolution. Such sentiments were shared by small numbers, but these were the persons who constructed empire and those who would dismantle it.

This dramatic and suggestive way of describing the historical problem has been made to introduce the difficulties – and to warn against the dangers – of treating 'decolonization' as a process, which the name etymologically implies; a process either initiated or controlled by the French, which the prefix implies, The term is useful as a sweeping generalisation and as, in Max Weber's phrase, an intellectual construct. But history is concerned both with the uniqueness of the moment – 'the erupting event' – and with particular attitudes – the 'climate of opinion' – by which such generalisations are tested.

French decolonisation was marked much more by turbulence, by the onrush of opposing forces into a political vacuum, than that of other nations. Or, to put it other than in Newtonian metaphor, the near paralysis of the national government, the often impetuous action of colonial officials on the scene and the intensifying discontent of the local populations mark French decolonisation more pronouncedly than that of any other such national retreat. Raymond Aron, one of the most acute observers of the modern French cultural scene, described the 'process' best in one of several lectures he gave at Harvard University in 1957. Aron declared:

Once indecision and unauthorized acts together had brought on the explosion, the official slogan became "hold on" (just as at Verdun).[2]

This historical condition of ineptness and obstinacy certainly mark the end, yet the overall history of the phenomenon of French imperialism is not so characterised. In retrospect, what seems so obvious is this correlation: the lack of popular French concern about empire was matched by the lack of lasting effect of the colonial act. It is true that imperialism left a heavier imprint on the colonised than on the coloniser, but the quality of that imprint – its enduring distinctiveness, if there is one – still remains a matter of contemporary scholarly debate, 30 years after the French overseas empire disappeared from the maps of the world.

What is historically obvious is the limited duration of the intensity of modern French imperialism, those multiple acts of military intrusion and diplomatic action by which the French established 'formal empire', claimed possession of territory beyond the seas. Between 1830, when the French sent an expeditionary force into Algeria, and 1912, when they established a protectorate over Morocco, the French extended their domain around the world, an activity lasting less than 100 years – and shorter in scale than that if the most intensive period of modern imperialism, once broadly called the 'scramble for Africa and Oceania', is considered. This activity occurred during the early years of the Third Republic, dramatically beginning in 1881, the year in which Tunisia was placed under French control.

Much less time was required for the dismantling of the resultant empire. From 1946 until 1960, from the first threatening militant opposition of the nationalists in Indochina to the peaceful appearance of republics among the former colonies of French West Africa, all but the smallest parts of the colonial empire were lost to France – or given up by that nation.

The causes and effects of overseas expansion and dominion cannot be assigned to any single group, arranged according to any single purpose. The French colonial empire was not actually the construction of conniving or evil men any more than it was the work of lofty visionaries. Nor did its crashing conclusion result in complete destruction or even extensive disruption of all that had been there in thought and in fact. About all that can be offered as sweeping, yet irrefutable, generalisation is this: neither cause nor effect of empire made the world at large much better or much worse.

Today, the French presence in Africa and Asia is almost totally a matter of the past, yet not so long gone in years as in attitudes and values. What has been left behind, besides roads, buildings, language, political and educational institutions, is no nostalgia and little resentment for that extended moment when the French could speak highly of their colonial 'vocation'.

1 Historical Conditions

The gilded statue commissioned for the 1931 International Colonial Exposition now stands on a small island of grass and shrubbery in the 12th arrondissement of Paris where it also stares out in loneliness at a busy intersection of a city whose population is engaged in worldly affairs no longer of an imperial nature. The statue is the only sculpted allegory in Paris to the *génie coloniale*, that imagined distinctive quality of the French colonial effort. Unlike Londoners, Parisians are not reminded by art of their days of imperial grandeur – other than those, of course, marked out by the greatest of French empire builders, Napoleon Bonaparte, who had been principally interested in moving over the European continent, not across the seas.

Aside from occasional appearances in the popular adult comic strips, the *bandes déssinées*, colonial images and settings now attract little attention. Nor did they even in the bright light of European expansion, that time in the early twentieth century when the French empire, consisting of 4 776 000 square miles of territory, or 9.3% of the globe's land surface (with metropolitan France included), was second only in cartographic majesty to the British Empire with its 12 191 000 square miles or 23.9% of the world's real estate.

More than most others who raised the flag abroad, the French were inattentive to what was dramatically described as the course of empire. Inner-directed – the *politique de clocher*, or church steeple politics, was a popular metaphor suggesting what was the focus of so much of daily life for so many of the predominantly rural population – the affairs of the nation were primarily Continental when extended beyond the borders. Pronounced since the reign of Louis XIV, this European orientation was further marked – truly scarred – by the French defeat in the Franco-Prussian War of 1870. After that occurrence, politicians invoked a new geographic imperative: the need to keep the national vision fixed on the 'blue line of the Vosges', the mountains which ran between Alsace and Lorraine, territories annexed by the Germans as the spoils of war.

Moreover, there was no concerted imperial effort that either

5

quickly seized or long held public attention; it was only the occasional, spirited act – the *beau geste* of a military commander or a colonial administrator – which aroused momentary interest. If, as has been said, the British Empire was acquired in a 'fit of absence of mind', the French colonial empire was no more rationally assembled. Jules Harmand, an ardent imperialist whose *Domination et colonisation* (1910) was an influential justification of empire, stated that French colonial acquisition, when not undertaken to assure protection of existing territories, 'occurred more as a result of instinct and sentiment than of carefully thought out and debated reasons'.[1]

Yet the imagined totality of it all – the appearance on the map – had a certain appeal to an ardent group who even before General Charles de Gaulle popularised the notion of *grandeur* argued that France would be great or would not be at all. These individuals might have smiled with satisfaction at the indirect commentary on French imperialism made by Joseph Conrad's Marlowe in *The Heart of Darkness* when he viewed the map of Africa and then said that 'there was a deuce of a lot of blue' appearing on it. Such colouration was comforting to those Frenchmen who knew that their nation was no larger than the state of Texas, itself part of a continental power which represented a new world order of things.

As the *Pax Americana* briefly reigned over a Europe recovering from war after 1945, the French witnessed and agonised over and fought against the dismantling of this imperial estate. Reluctant to accede to the wishes and demands of colonial nationalists anywhere, the postwar French governments were particularly determined to hold on to Indochina and Algeria, with consequent wars that were the most brutally long and costly of any fought in the era of decolonisation.

Now that painful unknotting experience is also behind the French. The end occurred less than 100 years after the beginning. The phenomenon itself, modern imperialism, was a late nineteenth-century affair, although it seems as if it ought to be placed further back in time because its special qualities and justifying explanations are so at variance with those which define domestic and inter-national behaviour in the contemporary world. The rhetoric (notions of 'civilizing mission'), the trappings (linen uniforms and pith helmets), the trade patterns (small family companies in French coastal cities with a handful of representatives abroad) all now have

a patina about them, appearing as out of place in modern France
as would be ivory elephants on a mantlepiece.

THE DEFINITION OF 'FRANCE OVERSEAS'

France d'Outre-Mer was a grandly designed name for a great number
of properties scattered around the world but that were never joined
in purpose or in organisation or in sentiment. In unrolling a cloth-
backed global map of that era, the contemporary viewer will find
France nicely situated in the centre of the world's rectangularised
surface with properly colour-coded lands, both large and small,
scattered from the central entity which the French call the *métropole*.

Across the Atlantic were the remnants of the first colonial empire,
the one in which Canada had been labelled *Nouvelle France*. The
fishing islands of St Pierre and Miquelon, off the coast of Newfound-
land, comprised 93 square miles of land on which about 5000
inhabitants huddled. Farther south and much larger were Guadeloupe and Martinique, Caribbean islands, which were also northwest of French Guiana, on the northern coast of South America and
best known because it looks out to Devil's Island, the most infamous
of the French possessions.

Southward from France stretched the most impressive and
massive colonial units. There was French North Africa, based on
Algeria, acquired after a naval invasion in 1830, and the first
political element in what would become the second colonial empire.
To its east was Tunisia, dominated by the French as a 'protectorate'
through treaty arrangements first effected in 1881. And to the west
was Morocco, the land that caught the eye of Paul Matisse and was
immediately fixed brilliantly on canvas when that primly attired
artist visited that radiant place first in 1912, the year the French
signed another 'protectorate', this time with the government of the
sultan.

Below, beyond most of the sandy sea reaches of the Sahara, in the
savannah and the jungle, the French accumulated large pieces of
land that were eventually formed into even larger administrative
units. This was territory first touched upon by sailors from Dieppe
in the sixteenth century and, after the Napoleonic Wars, reoccupied
administratively. Géricault's famous painting, *The Raft of the
Medusa*, first exhibited at the Salon of 1819, was testimony to that

event, for the French ship Medusa had been wrecked off the West African coast as it brought military personnel to Senegal in 1816.

By the beginning of the new century this maritime disaster had been forgotten, while the subsequent wars of conquest had been glorified, as the hinterland into which the French marched from their positions along the coast of Senegal was integrated into a large administrative unit called French West Africa, with its federal capital at Dakar, situated on the crooked fingertip of land that points to Brazil. The military activity allowing this result had its own contrived romance, largely provided by the *Tirailleurs sénégelais*, those sharpshooters who wore bright red fez and who were enrobed in a reputation – generated by the French – for fearsome warrior behaviour. In the twentieth century, one of these *tirailleurs* appeared in sketched form as the symbol for a popular French breakfast food, Banania. The advertisement, which went through many renderings, offered the metropolitan French their most familiar vision of the colonial people that their government had charged itself to guide.

The second unit was French Equatorial Africa, its name designating its location, with its capital at Brazzaville, a small town on the Congo River, named after the great French explorer, Pierre Savorgnan de Brazza, who had acquired much of the Congo territory for the French. Then, he crossed the lower waist of Africa in the years 1896–98 with the help of African labour which bolted and unbolted a small steamer that plodded up the riverways when it was not carried piece-by-piece across the intervening land that led on to Fashoda, on the Nile, in the Sudan, where English pluck and the doggedness of the great Lord Kitchener forced the French, in a celebrated showdown of 1898, to withdraw from the fort they had but recently occupied. As the French left, they took with them all plans for empire on the banks of the Nile.

Nonetheless, the French did have a handful of territorial pieces eastward. They had occupied Dijoubti and a small portion of surrounding land on the Red Sea, beginning in 1884, and then, in 1896 naming the totality French Somaliland (in French: *Côte française des Somalis*), linked by rail with Addis Abba in Ethiopia. Off the coast was the 'Great Island' of Madagascar, which Frenchmen had occasionally trodden upon, with Fort Dauphin established in 1643 as a revitalising place on the maritime route to India. However, it was through two particularly nasty little colonial wars against the Merina kingdom, first in 1885 and then in 1896, that France established command over the island.

Many other islands with French flags fixed upon them abounded as one sailed from Dijoubti toward the Pacific. The Comoros, off the coast of Madagascar, as did Réunion (which reflecting home politics had also been called Bourbon and Bonaparte), and Mauritius (formerly the Ile de France) in the Indian Ocean, attested to the seaworthiness of previous French colonial intentions. Mauritius as the Ile de France merits special literary attention because it was on that 'blessed isle' that the notion of tropical romance was launched, with the beach, not the garden, there serving as an Edenic place in the now famous novel – required reading in many American university courses – *Paul et Virginie*, a tale of ill-fated, youthful love, written by Jacques Henri Bernardin de Saint-Pierre, who described the place, at the end of the eighteenth century, in colours of azure, purple and salad green. Far more prosaic were the small enclaves, the trading 'factories', on the cast coast of India, of which Pondicherry was the best known. These inconsequential places were all that remained of the territorial dreams of Joseph-François Dupleix (pronounced *pleks* according to the *Petit Larousse* dictionary) who had aspired to excel the English at company-sponsored empire there, but whose East India Company received little governmental support and collapsed in 1770, a few years after Dupleix's death in 1763.

In the late nineteenth century, a new French eastward thrust touched Southeast Asia, the area later to be called Indochina. The territories of Cochin-China, Annam and Tonkin – which now form Vietnam – along with Cambodia and Laos, all occupied by the French, were made into a federation in 1887. Although the French had developed interests in the region as early as the reign of Napoleon III (emperor between 1852–70), it was in 1879 that military conquest earnestly began and, at about the same time, that commercial interests intensified. With the territories under the authority of a governor-general, resident in a fine palace in Hanoi, the French colonial regime busied itself with police action against Chinese bandits, the 'Blag Flags', in the north, and with plans for economic improvement everywhere in the region. Army engineers undertook the most impressive and financially questionable of overseas railroad projects: the Transindochinese which ran 1735 miles along the coast and which occupied the years between 1898 and 1936 in construction. Indochina, more specifically, Cambodia, was also the place in which the young André Malraux, later a famous novelist and minister of culture during the presidency of Charles de Gaulle, was charged and fined in the 1920s for stealing art objects in the form of bas reliefs from a Buddhist temple wall that he, his wife and a collaborator had forcefully detached, not too far from the great structure of Anghor, the most celebrated of architectural works in the region and one frequently imitated in colonial expositions held in France.

Out in the South Pacific the French organised their Oceania. They had held the island of New Caledonia since 1853 which for 30 years, 1864–94, was a penal colony. Over a thousand miles eastward and projecting quite a different cultural image was French Polynesia, a cluster of islands and atolls. There are found the Marquesas, where the American novelist Herman Melville situated his own South Sea idyll, *Typee* (1846); and where, later, in 1929, the great German film director Friedrich Wilhelm Murnau, best known for his vampire film *Nosferatu* and then making the film *Tabu*, found the indigenous population to be 'like pictures of Gauguin come to life'.[2]

Paul Gauguin is buried there, but his paintings derive from his residence on another part of French Polynesia, Tahiti, which the artist lushly set apart from the rest of the world and thus greatly enriched the already accepted Western designation of that sea-lapped place as paradise. Hollywood realised the advantage of such a myth when films sparkled on the silver screens in the era of the Great Depression. Visual transport away from the bleakness of daily life to the sight, for an hour or so, of swaying palm trees and carefree Polynesians was the cinematic strategy that brought directors to Tahiti to film 'on location' many of the South Sea romances, of which *Mutiny on the Bounty* (1935) is the most famous.

Small islands and extensive continental land masses, the territorial possessions of France were found all around the world, yet were so scattered, so disparate in environment and culture, that they could hardly become the empire *en bloc* that imperialists urged that they be at the end of the nineteenth century. 'Empire' was a verbal convenience, perhaps a shibboleth uttered to conjure up what was not there.

"Why 'Empire', why 'Our Empire'?" asked J. L. Gheerbrandt in his *Notre Empire: un univers, un idéal*, published in 1943:

Empire because what strikes one in considering these worlds in the World is that they unite nearly everything that one knows of the living Universe, of its natural and spiritual forces, so as to create a whole, one and indivisible.[3]

There was no unity beyond the metaphysical one just described. Nothing came together: there was no single governmental agency that was responsible for overseeing all colonial activities; individual colonies were administered differently – but seldom with any consideration given to local indigenous needs. The Cartesian thought on which the French prided themselves never was applied to colonial affairs, conducted to outward appearance without rhyme or reason.

But appearances, particularly on a grand scale, are frequently deceptive. Some Frenchmen certainly knew what they were about, even if most of their countrymen did not and did not even care. Owners of uncompetitive enterprises, like candle manufacture and silk cloth, leaned on empire as if it were an economic crutch preventing them from falling into bankruptcy.[4] New businesses, the Michelin tyre company, for instance, found natural resources readily accessible through indigenous labour working on newly created plantations in Indochina. The military, without glorious wars to be waged at the end of the nineteenth century, found room for promotion in the expanses of Africa, where a bold foray into disputed territory might be favourably interpreted by a minister at home and therefore lead to another set of *galons*. The wasted – the poet Arthur Rimbaud comes to mind – and the disadvantaged – young men without good employment opportunities at home – might find a nook or cranny in a tropical environment where they were regarded as *petits blancs* but where they might pretend to be *broussards*. And the romantic in spirit, of which there were many, could rejoice in their imagined-to-be primeval environment removed from bourgeois convention and urban configuration. Thus, Hubert Lyautey, first resident-general in Morocco, referred to that land as 'our Far West'; while Lieutenant-Colonel Alexandre Moll in a letter written as he was on an expedition in Equatorial Africa, exclaimed: 'Ah! If I were not making the effort to be useful and to lead a life of manly and vigorous activity, how unhappy I would be!'[5]

Empire thus rewarded some for their attention. As for the rest of the population, it was occasionally diverted by a dashing scene sketched on the cover of the popular geographical journal *Le Tour du Monde*, as it was occasionally alerted during a parliamentary debate over colonial finances. However, there was one extended moment when national attention was indeed focused on empire, not empire overseas but its surrogate laid out in Paris.

The International Colonial Exposition of 1931 was the grandest celebration of empire the French ever prepared. In quality of arrangement and in architecture, as in popular appeal, it far exceeded the earlier British variant, the British Empire Exposition of 1924. Beautifully arranged in the Bois de Vincennes, overseen by Hubert Lyautey, whose organisational genius was here displayed at its best, the exhibition was an empire in miniature – and something more than that. It suggested an order, unity and purpose that the real empire, scattered over the globe, never acquired. Here was displayed the empire *en bloc*. Here also was an empire at peace: harmony celebrated in the art works that abounded, and which expressed what was desired, not what was achieved. Commentary on the massive bas-relief which adorned the outer walls of the Museum of Colonies confirmed the significance of this artistic unity. 'Nothing comparable exists in all the history of sculpture', wrote the critic Gaston Varenne. He then described the work as an 'immense sculpted "tapestry"', or, if one prefers, a vast movie film in relief. . .'. The title of this monumental work (1200 square metres), designed by the sculptor Alfred Janniot, was: 'The Contribution of the Overseas Territories to the Mother Country and to Civilization'.[6]

The facade of the museum, along with the temporary structures laid out in the Bois de Vincennes, were the forms of an empire about which French colonialists dreamed but never awakened to.

The exposition was a dazzling success; however, memory of it faded just a few years later when World War II broke out, the war which destroyed France and undermined its colonial empire. So vast in scope, so devastating in effect was this first truly global war that it has often been singled out as the dreadful *primum mobile* of decolonisation, the force that shook all European pretences and shattered all imperial illusions, that revealed to the colonial peoples the flimsiness, as well as the inequity, of the European enterprise.

Ever recognising that big events erupt from multiple causes, historians are still in need of key terms, compelling analogies or metaphors by which to explain in brief compass such widespread occurrences. Therefore, they frequently turn to the meteorological, not the historical, for the proper element to describe what was happening: a storm brewing, a wind blowing, a volcano erupting, a tide sweeping in.

None of these terms, however, seems appropriate for the historical condition of the French colonial empire. Rather, the metaphor should come from engineering, a particularly appropriate field of comparison for a nation that was crudely constructing a colonial empire at the very time Gustave Eiffel was constructing with incredible finesse the tower that bears his name and that still stands as a glorious expression of French ingenuity.

The French colonial empire was structurally unsound; it was flawed. Although the French colonial theorists tried to design a solid structure, to bring the colonies together as a single mass, *en bloc*, they never got beyond expressions of hope and good intention. What resulted was ill-joined, pieces and parts never strongly welded together. There was no single administrative authority in charge of the entire enterprise; there was no solid public support behind the endeavour; there was no well-designed programme of development to improve it all. Like the Third Republic, the government that was almost coterminous with it, the French colonial empire functioned but did not function well.

Moreover, the consonance that characterised the British colonial effort – a strong alignment between Empire and Conservative thought, between Crown and overseas authority, between national mission and imperial objectives – this did not exist in France. That fusion of king, nation and empire in popular English thought, an arrangement which remains visible today along the length of the Mall between Admiralty Arch and Buckingham Palace in London, had no equivalent in France.

France was primarily a continental nation. Its so-called 'natural boundaries' were part of significant historical geography: the Pyrennes and the earlier rivalry with Spain, the highlands of Savoy and the overland route to Italy, the Rhine River and the continuing 'German problem', the North Sea which brought France close to and separated it from England.

It was toward these boundaries and borders which were hundreds of kilometres, not thousands of miles, away from Paris that most French politicians looked with concern. In terms of the balance-of-power theories favoured at the time, the French colonial empire was a makeweight to be added to the scale of European politics and, in the twentieth century, to global politics. With the advent of new political forces on the world scene – the United States, Germany, Japan and then the Soviet Union – France diminished relatively. More than one French politician warned that without its colonial empire France would be the Belgium, perhaps even the Switzerland, of the future.

Only when they found themselves in something of a romantic mood would French politicians refer to their nation as the *petit pré carré* (the little square field). For the imperialists, France was more aptly seen as a hexagon outwardly expanding so as to become a meaningfully proportioned monolith in a world of large structures. This desired condition was also deemed to be a historical fact. 'French expansion is an enduring and permanent phenomenon,' wrote Pierre Lyautey, nephew of Hubert Lyautey, in his popular study, *L'Empire colonial français*, published in 1931.[7] Yet, just three decades after these words were printed, the French colonial empire no longer existed.

Today France retains overseas a few island places, some small continental edges, what one French critic has described as a 'confetti empire'. Scooped up and transported to France, all of it could be comfortably arranged within the nation's continental boundaries.

Empire is now only a historical term in France, and one that does not receive the attention it does in Great Britain. Even the Museum of Colonies, the one permanent building left in place from the International Colonial Exposition of 1931, no longer serves that function. It is now a museum for African and Oceanic art. Historically conscious as perhaps no other people are, the French have largely forgotten about their recent colonial past. Yet the gilded statue in the 12th arrondissement, which indeed stood before the Museum of Colonies when that building was so proudly named, still firmly holds its trident, a reminder, should anyone care to notice, that *France d'Outre-Mer* was at one time a favoured phrase, an intended place.

THE COLONIAL SPIRIT

In the early years of the new French colonial empire, the petty bourgeois spirit, a continual subject of foreign delight, was manifested in a minor legal matter raised in Algiers. In 1850 a French dentist named Dupire wished to place a plaque advertising his practice on the facade of a neighbouring mosque. The chief architect of the city recommended to the prefect of the region that the request be denied, as earlier had been a similar one for a furniture shop, on the basis of its inappropriateness for a 'religious temple'. There the matter rested, today only marked as item '4M22' in the folders of the Archives d'Outre-Mer housed in Aix-en-Provence.

Yet on a larger scale of historical interpretation this incident reaches into later history in an emblematic way: it offers in its particularity a set of general characteristics of the French overseas enterprise.

First, nothing imperial, rhetoric excepted, was ever grand-scaled. The frequent complaint coming from the imperialists was that everything was undertaken as if *petits paquets*, little packages, bits-and-pieces. Not only was the empire so acquired, but it was also so developed. People, capital and planning were all in short supply. Large and diversified financial or business establishments were infrequent. The individual merchant, the lawyer, the school teacher or the dentist, was the principal residential colonist. Only in Algeria, which was what the French called a *colonie du peuplement*, was there a considerable residential population, and it was concentrated along the coast in a few major cities like Algiers and Oran or was sparsely scattered in the countryside, where it was family-based, farm-situated, long-settled. Elsewhere, the colonist was far less evident than the colonialist. Even in the interwar period, when French families started to migrate in some number to West Africa, and the cultural contours began to change – hairdressers, pastry shops appeared, for instance – the colonial environment was hardly more bracing. *Soudainété*, 'Sudanness', was jokingly named and defined as a psychological condition of lethargy. That sense of cultural inertia was captured sardonically by Albert Camus in his famous existentialist novel, *The Plague*. At the beginning of the work, he describes the colonial city of Oran, where the plot takes place, this way: 'Treeless, glamorless, soulless, the town of Oran ends up by seeming restful and, after a while, you go complacently asleep there'.[8]

The basic demographic fact is this: the French colonial empire was essentially populated only temporarily by administrators and military personnel.

Second, the dentist's request demonstrates an insensitivity to the local culture, its mores and values. Later French critics would praise the richness of Moslem culture in North Africa, just as artists like Delacroix had by then romanticised it as sensual, sinewy, forceful. In a less artful way, the intended plaque, to be inscribed in the French language, suggests a graver misinterpretation of the Moslem world, that resulting from a spirit of condescension toward foreign cultures and the people who practised them.

Casting the world beyond the so-called 'West' in images that were exotic or quaint, mysterious or frightening, the French, like the other European imperialists, prided themselves on their advancements, on the rational and orderly way they considered they did things: kept their business ledgers, made their trains run, observed the world. At a time when column charts easily measured gross national product, and when the height of the Eiffel Tower was so measured against all the other tall stuctures ever erected, it was easy for the Frenchman of the late nineteenth century to assume that other cultures and other peoples were below his level of attainment.

All too seldom seeking appreciation of the culture he encountered, the French administrator, merchant or traveller dismissed what was there or tended to deprecate it. Even as sensitive a writer as the French novelist André Gide exhibited this attitude of disinterest or disrespect for the new mind of Africa. In his much discussed and cited study, *Voyage au Congo*, first published in 1927, Gide offers the equation, 'The less intelligent the white man is, the more stupid he thinks the black'. Yet some 60 pages after, or two months later in his account, he says of the black Africans:

Not that I think them capable of any but the slightest mental development; their brains as a rule are dull and stagnant – but how often the white man seems to make it his business to thrust them back into their darkness.[9]

The dismissal was all the easier because of the assimilationist theory by which the French buttressed their activities. French civilisation, certainly second to none, was often proclaimed to be above all by many of its proponents. In the colonial world such an assumption was a truism. It allowed a comfortable assumption of authority: a 'civilizing mission' to be carried abroad by a nation which pretended that it had inherited Rome's genius and which had invented its own universal concept of fraternity during the Revolution that began in 1789. This fusion of imagined administrative responsibility with proclaimed revolutionary purpose was the foundation of French colonial ideology. It proposed a social and political symmetry, a colonial world balanced by French legislation and institutions, by the French concept of citizenship, by the use of the French language. The very term, *France d'Outre-Mer*, 'Overseas France', was expressive of these sentiments. Underlying them, according to Alfred Fouillée, a popular French cultural analyst at the turn of the nineteenth century, was the belief 'that what makes us happy will make everyone happy, that all of humanity must think and feel as France does'.[10] Such thought urged its own political conclusions.

Until the late afternoon of French colonial empire, administrative assimilation held its appeal, an appeal found based in the revolutionary principle of 'a nation one and indivisible'. What France intended was a single global community, a nation of '100,000,000', to use the bold, round figure that was proclaimed in the interwar period. While English political theory provided the concept of the trust and, hence, of the possible disassembling of empire into autonomous or independent units, the French did not. According to Arthur Girault, one of the most careful analysts of French colonial institutions in the early twentieth century and a professor of political economy at the University of Poitiers, the ideal of assimilation 'is not separation, but, on the contrary, an increasingly intimate union between the colonial and the metropolitan territory.... The colonies are theoretically considered to be a simple extension of the soil of the mother country'.[11] This ideological concern with unity would be a major problem of negotiations in the decade of decolonisation. It was affirmed as late as 1944 at the Brazzaville Conference when the French Provisional Government of General Charles de Gaulle declared autonomy and independence unacceptable.

Third, the incident of the dentist may be viewed as visible evidence of the petty or small scale of French interest in the colonial empire. Protagonists regularly lamented the fact that the French private sector was purse-pinching wherever overseas enterprise was concerned. Always persistent was the call for *mise en valeur*, the economic development of the colonial empire. Only after World War II, when technology replaced administration as the desirable objective of colonial affairs, did the French pour large sums of money regularly into development.

The world of international cartels and transoceanic financial duplicity that Lenin imagined and translated into his remarkable study, *Imperialism, The Highest Stage of Capitalism* (1918), did not disturb the drowsy streets of Dakar, Senegal or the small shop talk in Point-à-Pitre, Guadeloupe. Revisionist historical theory, seeking to temper the wrought iron of Marxist interpretation, argues, and compellingly, that the newer capitalist enterprises in France were not primarily or even strongly colonial-directed in their effort to dispose of surplus capital or goods. It was the collection of uncompetitive businesses which were small-scaled, out-dated, often manufacturing products out of line with modern industry, that were the principal ones that sought in empire a protected place, a sort of haven for those weary of trafficking in the competitive market.[12]

Such colonial activity, as briefly described here, was not bold, was not even mildly disruptive of national patterns of behaviour. As a generally uncostly diversion, it created its own irony, that expressed by Jules Ferry, the most ardent of imperialists who, briefly watching a belly-dancer at the 1889 Parisian Exposition, suggested that that was what most Frenchmen though empire was all about.

From 1830, the year in which the French first moved militarily into Algeria, until 1942, when General Charles de Gaulle established his provisional government there, colonial affairs were seldom of major national consequence. Only as the nation's overseas territories fell – or pulled – away did the French government and the French people pay much attention to the issue of 'empire'. Yet even in the face of that anguish, which was the unexpected loss of life, the unwanted expenses and terrorism at home as well as in Algeria, the French did not as a nation, as a people, engage in a major colonial debate, make empire a compelling issue of the ballot box. For the Third, for the Fourth and for the Fifth Republic, *France d'Outre-Mer* remained a secondary matter.

2 An Empire Peaceful and Disturbed

A French naval recruitment poster from the interwar period, now preserved in the *Musée de Publicité* in Paris, shows two bright-eyed young sailors standing on an island protected by a French man-of-war riding serenely at anchor and surrounded by tropical copiousness: one sailor is holding a large bunch of bananas, the other is admiring a parrot, while at their feet is crouched a contented island woman to the left of whom is a monkey touching a pineapple. The depicted scene was of a particular colonial reality, yet far removed from the eventful one that had greeted Jean Merlin, French Governor-General of Indochina, as he was being driven from a banquet in Canton, China. Merlin was the intended victim of a bomb attack by a Vietnamese nationalist. Although he escaped injury, several Frenchmen in his entourage died. This violence took place in 1924, some three years before the recruitment poster was printed, and some 3000 miles away from the idyllic island scene the poster presented.

The French colonial empire in the interwar era offered a variety of settings; generated praise and aroused anger, both abroad and at home, both in word and deed. Almost everyone who engaged in colonial affairs recognised the particular time and the general condition as transitional; change was widely expected, but neither dramatic nor radical change. The key terms best representing the thinking and the mood of most of the leaders in the colonial world are: reform, development, respect. This general desire for improvement that would better the economy and the social and cultural relationships of the diverse peoples placed in what was soon called the 'colonial situation' occasionally was translated into violent protest, notably in Indochina, but was more frequently translated into political discussion and literary expression: a lot was spoken and written about the condition of the 'empire', the term itself newly popular in the interwar period but more suggestive of aspiration than reality.

19

While primarily centred in France and particularly in Paris where the cultural attraction was always greatest, the debate over the shape the empire should take was widespread, and it engaged nearly as many of the colonised as the colonisers. Nowhere outside of France was it more significant and striking in effect than in Vietnam, where a pronounced literary change occurred, that of the growing use in the early twentieth century of *quoc-ngu*, the romanised script adaptation of the Vietnamese language.

Initiated by Portuguese missionaries, *quoc-ngu* abolished the complexities of Vietnamese characters and thereby allowed the easy adaptation of the language to printed form. The French authorities supported writing in *quoc-ngu* in the early days of colonial domination as a means of introducing the population to the romanised script of Western languages and thus to French itself, which the colonial administration had wanted to make the dominant language. By the beginning of the twentieth century, however, it was clear that this French instructional effort had failed but that *quoc-ngu* was widely gaining in use and influence, with a profusion of newspapers, literary journals and books in that language occurring during the interwar period. (According to one historian, some 9000 such publications for the period 1912–40 are found in the collection of the French National Library in Paris.) *Quoc-ngu* had become the vehicle for a sort of linguistic nationalism conveying a poetry of protest, historical studies devoted to the pre-colonial period and essays urging modernisation.[1]

Yet, this impressive literary development is the notable exception to the rule. French remained the *lingua franca* of the small number of educated in the French colonial empire. 'To speak,' remarked the radical Martinquan author Frantz Fanon in his book *Peau noir, masques blancs* (translated in 1967 as *Black Skin, White Masks*), 'is to assume a culture, to support the weight of a civilization.'[2] While Fanon was critical of this linguistic burden, the use of French was the principal means by which an African or an Asian might enter the intellectual domain – scientific as well as literary – of the West and might communicate with a French audience. French was also the means by which to overcome one element of the alienation created by a cultural system transposed from abroad. As the Martiniquan mother in Léon Damas's poem 'Hoquet' exclaims in protest to her son who is speaking Creole:

I told you you must speak French
the French of France
the Frenchman's French
French French.[3]

Like his fellow countryman, Frantz Fanon, Damas was critical of
this linguistic-cultural condition, the resulting 'zebra striping of my
mind', as Fanon put it. Yet for him, for Fanon and for all others
engaged in the colonial debate, French remained the language of
discourse.

THE INTERWAR PERIOD: A NEW DEBATE AND A NEW PERSPECTIVE

The debate – perhaps 'discussion' is a better word – that occurred
in the interwar period was two-sided and double-pronged. Political
order and economic development were made the chief justifications
for empire; political oppression and economic exploitation were the
two chief objections registered against it. The ongoing conflict
between the two sets of conditions was both verbal and physical:
parliamentary debates and manifestos, uprisings and strikes.

Yet this was no turbulent environment threatening to change in
radical manner the colonial situation. Introspection and self-doubt
were certainly the two contrasting moods evident at home and
among those who were concerned with colonial matters. However,
reform was their common objective. For all the praise heaped on
empire by its proponents, and despite the embarrassment about it
sensed by some intellectuals, there seemed to be little certainty as
to what would be the course of empire. The movement – it was not
so calculated or organised to merit being called a process – toward
decolonisation began in the last moments of colonial confidence,
those immediately following World War I. Yet, during this time,
confidence in the continuation of the empire was still strong; the
major doubt was over what empire would become. Pierre Lyautey
concluded his general survey, *L'Empire colonial français*, with a
question: 'What are the one hundred million Frenchmen going to
do?'[4] Expansion was over, Lyautey asserted; the current issue was
one of application, what ought to be made of the colonies in order
to form an empire with unity of purpose and function.

Most others who at the time turned their attention to the construction of a new ideology of empire argued similarly, with their key word now being responsibility, not power. Albert Sarraut, certainly the most famous colonial theorist of the time and a politician who had served as governor-general of Indochina and minister of colonies, expressed this responsibility eloquently, yet in typical French colonial idiom, in a speech he made on 19 July 1930:

Mandatory of civilization, supported by the power of human solidarity, the colonizer could not without falsifying his mission and destroying his right to authority, elude those moral obligations that aroused him and urged him on in the first place.[5]

If not out of discomfort, then certainly out of an awareness of a need for change, men like Sarraut and Lyautey sought the reorganisation and the redirection of colonial empire. They were seeking accommodation to a newly reapportioned world where the geographic sweep of imperialism was no longer considered a noble national gesture.

THE EFFECTS OF WORLD WAR I

The World War had unsettled empire, weakening its ideological bases just as it weakened the power of the nations which held the largest colonial empires. The term 'expansion', which implied both brute force and the right to domination – the 'will' to empire – had no place in the revised political dictionary. If few French colonial theorists were desirous of accepting the new vocabulary of the American president, Woodrow Wilson, who offered the imperative 'make the world safe for democracy' and who proposed the principle of 'self-determination of nations', none was willing to oppose the language publicly.

From the mutually endured wartime experience came an acceptance of international responsibility, at least the formal expression of obligations that transcended national interest. It was a concept of international trust, of responsibility supposedly conferred on the nations of the West because of their advanced state, that now directed the colonial effort. In theory, a temporary trust was assigned to the 'civilized' nation for the well-being of the 'backward' territory.[6]

The French in effect adapted the famous term of the British colonial theorist, Lord Frederick Lugard, who defined that term in the title and contents of his book *The Dual Mandate in Tropical Africa*, first published in 1922. Lugard spoke of the need to develop the colonial regions economically for the benefit of all the world and to bring to these regions the blessings of civilisation. As interpreted by Albert Sarraut in his *La Mise en valeur des colonies* ('The Development of the Colonies'), published in the same year as Lugard's work and certainly one of the most influential works on colonialism ever written in French, the idea was much the same. Claiming that French colonial policy 'fundamentally begins with the great idea of human solidarity', Sarraut proceeded to argue:

> Colonizing France does not only work for itself; its advantage is confounded with the world's advantage; its efforts must be as beneficial to the colonies as to itself, for there France assures economic betterment and human development.[7]

In these words at least, global need supplanted national self-interest. Thus, the ideology of empire acquired both a new respectability and a new vulnerability. Imperial behaviour was, to some still uncertain degree, answerable to the world community, of which the colonised peoples were now recognised as a part.

This change was also evident in a new international institution which itself bore the name 'mandate', being in fact the particular source from which Lugard drew the term. Although not the original idea of Woodrow Wilson, it is one that he fostered. The political mandate was, above all else, a legal solution to a pressing political problem.

Among the spoils of war were the shattered remains of both the Ottoman and German empires. The fate of the German colonial empire was a potential embarrassment. The Germans had joined in the hymns of praise about the 'white man's burden'; they were co-colonialists playing the same game abroad as were the French and the British. To divest Germany of its colonies after that nation's defeat, therefore, was an act that required more than the old, crude assertion that 'to the victor go the spoils'. Accordingly, Germany was found to be morally wanting. Albert Sarraut provided the clearest explanation of this judgement:

> The high moral reason for this dispossession is the German colonial indignity, an indignity all the more appalling as the intellectual superiority which prevails in this nation was accompanied by a total disdain of all morality in colonial affairs.[8]

Sarraut then cited the argument of the French minister of colonies, Henry Simon, who said that Germany had been deprived of its colonies in the name of human rights, of the 'oppressed races'.

In an indirect but obvious way, this line of argument put all the colonial powers in an imaginary court of international justice, where the well-being of the indigenous population and the responsibility of the coloniser to assure it might be tried.

The mandate system reinforced such internationalisation but, again, more in theory than in practice. The mandate system was a means of administering the former possessions of the Ottoman and German empires without placing them directly into the category of colonies. The League of Nations chose the mandatory power, in every instance, whether a colonial power or, in the case of Australia, part of a colonial system. The mandatory was, according to Article 22 of the League charter, responsible and accountable for assisting the peoples under its charge, to be prepared to enter the modern world on their own. Here was, in reworked idiom, the old colonial of tutelage, a temporary arrangement whereby the more advanced would aid those culturally disadvantaged to self sufficiency.

Nevertheless, in practice the mandatory powers absorbed the mandated territories into their own colonial systems, while international surveillance of their activity was of a minimal, even inconsequential nature. In this manner, France gained control over Lebanon and Syria in the Near East and over a portion of the Cameroons in West Africa. As more than one historian has said, the French empire was enlarged as a result of World War I but outfitted in different disguise.[9]

What is probably most important about the mandate system is its ideological effect on the general history of decolonisation because of its internationalisation of colonial affairs through the principle of accountability to the League of Nations. While it is true that the French, no more than any other of the mandatories, were seriously

disturbed by the arrangement or anxious to fulfill its strict obligations, the establishment of the mandates system did further sensitise
the colonial enterprise to outside opinion, an unmeasurable but not
unimportant consideration in an age when information was being
more widely circulated through film, radio and popular journals.
World affairs were then more quickly reported, and international
opinion did have some effect on governmental behaviour. Considering this development many years later, after the end of the Algerian
war in which he had been a field commander, General André
Beaufre, wrote in his essay *Strategy for Tomorrow*, appearing in an
English edition in 1974, that media-expressed public opinion had
caused 'isolated local wars', such as those in Algeria or Vietnam, to
have 'sizeable moral repercussions around the world'.[10]

THE CONTINUING POLITICAL DEBATE

In a land of such political diversity and intensity as France, the new
colonial debate was not marked by severe differences in tone or in
content. This undisturbing, rather balanced condition was in part
the result of new international concerns and problems raised by the
appearance of Mussolini and Hitler on the political scene and in
greater part the result of domestic concerns in the 1930s, particularly the effects of the Depression and the disturbances caused by
French militant groups on the political Right. Furthermore, the very
existence of the empire, its simply being there, had heavy effect.
Rather like Atlas, but without his great strength, the French nation
had shouldered a colonial empire and hence an international
problem that it could not put down except through great effort, even
if divestment of empire had been considered a good objective.

What was most interesting in the debate was what was said on
the Left of the political spectrum. The Left in France had long
been ambivalent about empire. The Socialist Party had remained
inspired, even after his death in 1914, by Jean Jaurès, who had been
the most influential socialist and a reformer, not a revolutionary in
colonial matters. Although Jaurès opposed colonialism in principle,
he resigned himself to the fact that France had a colonial empire.
He therefore argued that the empire should only be ended after its
administrators had prepared the colonial peoples for independence.
This argument was but a variation of the old notion of *mission*

civilisatrice and a variation supported by Jaurès' successor, the most prominent Socialist of the interwar period, Léon Blum. As late as 1946, Blum declared:

> In our republican doctrine colonial possession does not reach its final goal and find its true justification until the day that it comes to an end, and that is to say, the day on which the colonial people has been rendered fully capable as an emancipated people of governing itself.[11]

However, Blum was constantly critical of French colonial rule. It was the hypocrisy and cruelty of what he saw that aroused his anger.

In a series of articles he wrote for the party newspaper, *Le Populaire*, in July 1927, he expressed his profound discontent with the prevailing colonial situation. 'Work and poverty,' he proclaimed, 'there's the law of life such as we go out to preach and apply in the name of a superior civilization.' He granted that colonial products were necessary for the world economy; thus he was in accord with Sarraut. But he complained of the servile nature of the work imposed by the French, and he worried about its possible implications.

> We run the risk of turning against us both that which subsists of the barbarian in the native and that which has grown in them of human nobility, which is to say the spirit of hate and the spirit of justice, the call for compassion and the call for revenge.

If there is a summary statement to be offered about the Socialist position on the colonial empire, it would be one that stressed the need to conclude the enterprise as quickly and honourably as possible so that a solidarity of interests – again the words of Blum in his speech of 1946 – would develop, that would allow both parties to the colonial act 'to unite freely'.

The official French Communist objection to imperialism was constructed of a different fabric, the one manufactured in the Soviet Union.[12] The different textures and tones in which Marxist thought was expressed in the early twentieth century never seriously altered the famous dialectical process: change through conflict. Some form of social struggle was deemed inevitable. Marxist theorists who gave their attention to the colonial situation knew it would be a violent

one before European power was removed. They were able to assure
continuity to theory and to strengthen it by equating the struggle of
the oppressed colonial peoples with their colonial overlords to the
struggle of the proletariat with their capitalist employers. The
mutual term was 'exploitation', a process carried out in both locales
for the same purpose: particular and therefore selfish economic
advantage.

Imperialism was stripped of any of its outer glitter by its Marxist-
Leninist critics who found it to be nothing more than a crass affair
of economics. Much of this argument had already been expressed
in French by Paul Louis in his work *Le Colonialisme*, published in
1905. It was refined into an intended global policy at the Second
Congress of the Communist International of 1920 and upheld by
Lenin. The policy called for a united effort between the proletarian
parties of the industrialised world and the bourgeois nationalist
movements in the other parts of the world, principally in those
regions under colonial rule. This strategic alliance disturbed ideological purists who desired no concourse, however politically convenient, with the bourgeois.

The insistence on adherence to the principles and policies laid out
by the Congress was a matter that quickly caused a split in the
French Socialist Party, with the majority of its membership voting
in support of the policies adopted by the Communist International
at the Socialist Party convention held in Tours, France, in December, 1920. Blum rallied a minority together which retained the
party's title, while the majority created the French Communist
Party, in league with Russia's revolution, not that of France.

Nonetheless, the new French Communist Party was anything but
doctrinaire in colonial matters. It both vigorously condemned and
remained studiously silent, the particular behaviour of the moment
dependent on perceived political advantages and shifts in Soviet
policy. At its annual party congress in 1926, a resolution was passed
to give support 'to the revolutionary movements directed against
French imperialism'. But during the years between 1935 and 1938,
when France had signed a defensive pact with the Soviet Union and
when the Popular Front government, based on Socialist and Communist parliamentary cooperation, was in power, the Communist
leadership asked only that French colonial policy be 'investigated',
not excoriated.

On no occasion was that unthreatening stance more clearly

assumed than in the address given by the party chief, Maurice Thorez, at the annual party meeting in 1937. Entitled 'France of the Popular Front and its Mission in the World', the speech contained denunciations of Mussolini's invasion of Ethiopia and of Japan's of China, but France's global position was only discussed in terms of the nation's need to find support among the popular masses of all countries.[13] The colonial empire was a subject conspicuous by its absence in that address.

Earlier, however, before Hitler menaced all, Communists had used the official vocabulary imported from Moscow to denounce France's colonial activities. This was particularly true during the Rif War, a quasi-feudal rebellion of an able tribal chief named Abd-el-Krim in Spanish Morocco to which both France and Spain responded with military engagement, beginning in 1925. The rhetorical efforts of the French Communist Party in favour of the Rifians were praised as a 'brilliant campaign' by the Communist International. The Communists employed their imperatives, variants of the classic admonitions of Marx. The headlines of the party newspaper, *L'Humanité*, exclaimed: 'French and Rifian workers, fraternize!' and 'Soldiers fraternize! Imperialists, get out!' Jacques Doriot, a Communist deputy at the time, suggested the establishment of a form of solidarity quite different from that proposed by Albert Sarraut. In a speech, he stated that the French peasants could 'not live with the exploitation of their Arab brothers'.[14]

Riots elsewhere, as in Indochina in 1930, and oppressive official policy, as in Syria and Tunisia around the same time, brought from both Socialists and Communists complaints and cries for change. Intellectuals, like the novelist André Malraux, found a mild irony in the fact that Thorez's major party speeches were grouped together in a book entitled, *Une politique de grandeur française*.

Both parties did advocate reform for the present. Hope of that occurring was high in parts of the colonial world when the Popular Front government took power in 1936. 'Never was the Algerian people so unanimous in its hopes,' later wrote the Algerian nationalist Ferhat Abbas of this moment in colonial history.[15] Marius Moutet, Socialist minister of colonies in 1936, planned reform. He envisioned an economic development through state aid to all parts of the colonial empire, 'a big program of small projects', as he described it, but the description was only met with parliamentary lack of support. Politically, Moutet sponsored the Blum-Violette bill, drawn up by the former governor-general of Algeria, Maurice Violette, which would have increased the number of French citizens among the Algerian population and thus would have liberalised the political rule of the colony. At the same time, a group of reform-minded Moroccans, anxious to gain some control over their own political destiny, had drawn up a 'Plan of Reforms' before the advent of the Popular Front government. Not seeking to abolish French sovereignty, the plan did call for a liberalisation of governmental control, the introduction of a single educational and judicial system for both French and Moroccans. Initially rejected by the French authorities, the Plan was again offered with enthusiasm to the new Popular Front government.

Neither set of reforms before the Blum government, its own for Algeria or that of the Plan for Morocco, got anywhere. Local opposition from French residents in the two territories was strong, including that strongly registered by the local branches of the Socialist Party, which were composed almost exclusively of Frenchmen. Moreover, the full effects of the Depression now fell on France and weakened any resolve to alter the colonial situation for fear of creating still more problems for the French populations there.

A CRITICAL REAPPRAISAL OF WESTERN VALUES

On the space scale of domestic French politics in the middle of the 1930s, the colonies had moved into a far-off orbit. Even so, they were being subtly realigned in the French global scheme of things. This change of position was the result of a new sentiment of cultural doubt and open-mindedness. The World War had left among its cadavers the previously strong body of late nineteenth-century thought, that combination of rationalism and the scientific attitude which had inspired the construction of the Eiffel Tower above the streets of Paris and the *Métro* below them, which had made Louis Pasteur an internationally famous immunologist and Emile Durkheim a founding father of modern sociology.

Where unbridled enthusiasm for scientific advancement had been the preeminent popular attitude before the war, reserve, even pessimism about human control of destiny was widely apparent after. Art fled to other levels of consciousness, away from outer reality to surrealism, for instance. Novelists and other writers journeyed away from France, principally to the Far East where they found comfort and a different form of reason in meditation. Perhaps the most significant French work of this particular movement is André Malraux's *Temptation of the West*, a dialogue published in 1921, in which the Chinese figure, Ling, writing of his experience in the West to A. D., a Frenchman journeying in the East, has the better argument – which is to say the worse view of what he is seeing.

Like Fernand Léger's famous painting from this time, 'Men of the City', Ling's view of Western civilisation is of a place and mode of behaviour that are disjointed, angular, tense, busy without graceful pattern. The missing element is serenity, a deep sense of self in repose in space. Malraux casts his verdict for the other side, when he allows Ling to say of Europeans:

> Your minds are of such a nature that they are capable of grasping only the fragmentary elements of life. You are carried away by the goals toward which you are incessantly aiming. You desire conquest? What do you find beyond your meager victories?[16]

Robert Delavignette, France's most thoughtful colonial administrator in the last years of empire, drew less striking cultural contrasts, but praised that form of human existence which was in harmony with the land. In his short book, *Les Paysans noirs*, published in 1931, he urges upon schoolchildren leaving for vacation in the colony of Upper Volta his own vision of Africa:

> Children . . . the white man hopes you will always smell the damp and sun-drenched grass and will always love, as he has loved, the gifts of your season of rains: the mountain sculpted and painted by the intense storm, the small marsh birds with their velvet-like plummage, the unexpected breeze that comes from afar and which goes still farther yet, and the seasonal clouds that uncover beneath their folds a sky so blue, so fine that the menace of a torrential rain is forgotten.[17]

In discussing the peanut industry in the region, Delavignette capitalised the word machine, providing it with a force or power that is rather exceptional in French style where few words are singled out for that authority. The 'Machine' in his perception of the colonial scene was an intruder and a boon, a disturber of the pastoral order and yet the means by which to improve the lot of the African. The ambivalence with which Delavignette assesses the forthcoming changes, with which he nostalgically regards what is still there of the African rural environment and what he hopefully anticipates is about to occur as improvement, was an exceptionally sensitive consideration of a transition many colonial administrators had seen and had pondered.

Amidst the unusual shapes and peculiar light of the colonial landscape, the colonial officer as foreign observer frequently found self-doubt along with new discovery. The older, brutal certainty that had marked the pages of pre-war works justifying imperialism now gave way to more thoughtful, balanced expression in which social change arising from understanding and respect replaced the forceful assertions of the need for expansion. The new formula was Delavignette's, 'humanism and leadership'.[18] It was an appealing formula, but one that never went very far from the printed page on which it first appeared.

NO CONCLUSION TO THE END OF AN ERA

Hesitant when not unresponsive to the call or the conflict directed to change, the French were nonetheless reformist in disposition. Now widely subscribing to the policy of 'association', an idea not dissimilar to the British notion of 'indirect rule', the French assumed a colonial attitude of cultural accommodation and political cooperation in place of the older one of domination. This attitude was subscribed to by the Minister of Colonies, Maurius Moutet, in a statement he made on 24 June 1936: 'A colonial system cannot survive unless it is operated from within by the natives who are supposed to benefit from it'.[19]

To assist in that effort the French refined their colonial methods, sought something of a colonial system or, at least, a systematic way of approaching colonial affairs. Administrative personnel were better trained, with the Colonial School, founded in Paris in 1889, assuming the primary responsibility for preparing administrators after World War I. Research institutes, of which the *Institut Pasteur* was the most famous because of its work in disease control, now appeared. Many anthropological studies were now undertaken, in some measure following the acclaimed work of Maurice Delafosse in Africa before and immediately after World War I, of which his study *Les noirs d'Afrique* (1922) was the most significant. Accompanying this effort was the request of at least one major colonial administrator, Governor-General Brevié of French West Africa, to seek some concordance between French and customary law by commissioning, in 1931, the preparation of a number of manuals on local African law.

Yet all such efforts were French initiated and directed, with the colonial peoples given little control over their own destinies. The local colonial officers, as Delavignette said of his own experience in West Africa immediately after World War I, '... had to be lonely and active chiefs'.[20] However, African chiefs, often appointed by the French, were in effect members of the colonial administration, Delavignette describing them as 'links' between the French administration and the African population. Jules Carde, the first French commissioner in the French portion of the mandated territory of the Cameroons, said of the regional chiefs newly established there, that they were 'above all else administrative organs'.[21]

Much was discussed and little was changed in that overseas world France unabashedly claimed as its own before World War II altered fact and opinion. Yet, even as it was evident that the political shape of the globe was being redefined, as the French watched with concern the growing power of Japan, were discomforted by the 'awakening' of the Moslem world, and were most aware of the threat of Hitlerian Germany across the Rhine, the proponents of empire were generally sanguine about the future. Georges Hardy, former director of the Colonial School, concluded his earth-sweeping study of modern colonisation with the argument that all evidence indicated that the global authority of Europe 'is far from having exhausted its resources of endurance'. He did qualify that statement with the phrase 'barring catastrophes'.[22]

Hardy's book was published in 1937, just two years before the outbreak of World War II.

3 The Changing Scene in the Colonial World

There is a certain charm now found in the reading of Ho Chi Minh's later reflections on his early revolutionary career. This future leader of Vietnamese resistance, first to the French and then to the Americans, and the first president of the Democratic Republic of Vietnam, much earlier found himself in France, where he initially remained removed from international affairs. Arriving in Paris in 1917, Ho was something of an apprentice in two new arts; a photographer's assistant where he retouched prints and a painter of sorts in what was to become a new worldwide industry: manufacture of folk art in places where it did not originate. In Ho's own words, he was 'a painter of "Chinese antiquities" (made in France!)'.[1]

These brief employments were end notes of a rather extensive travel programme which had occurred when Ho left Vietnam in 1911, where he had briefly been a teacher. As a cook on a French vessel plying the waters between Hanoi and Marseille, he travelled to Europe, briefly staying at Marseille, then moving on to London where he was a cook in a restaurant. Then, he moved on to Paris and the beginning of his long, remarkable career. There he schooled himself in modern politics and revolutionary ideology, after what he described becomingly as a modest beginning.

> The reason for my joining the French Socialist Party was that these "ladies and gentlemen" – as I called my comrades at that moment – had shown their sympathy toward me, toward the struggle of oppressed peoples. But I understood neither what was a party, trade-union, nor what was Socialism or Communism.[2]

Ho learned quickly, as did many others who became leaders of colonial groups and factions that attracted French attention more because of their threat to generate social disorder and political unrest than their potential to destroy the colonial order of things. Ho, certainly the most energetic and persistent among the naysayers in the interwar French colonial empire, was not certain in the early years of his involvement in Vietnamese politics of the success of his effort. He initially avoided the establishment of a Communist party there because he thought the population at the time ill-prepared for such an organisation. On the basis of such historical evidence, the contemporary critic will therefore not dismiss out of hand the statement made by Georges Hardy in his summary statement of the condition of empire, made in 1939, that although separatist agitation had appeared in some of the colonial areas, it had always been put down or accommodated by reform. He added, by way of reassurance, that there had been no lack of such territorial movements in European nations, 'but they all ended by being absorbed into the national unity'.[3] If Hardy is to be criticised, it is for his Eurocentric vision of the problems of the colonial world, of a failure to perceive the different nature and the intensity of the colonial grievance.

Such a perception may have even been assisted by the methods and modes of protest. As a meaningful historical generalisation, one may say that the French found returned, as if it had been contained in a poorly addressed envelope, what they had sent to the colonial territories: ideology and institutions. All historians agree that the movements of colonial protest, like the movements of national affirmation which quickly followed them, were of a syncretist nature: a combination of the local (tradition, religion, cultural values) and the imported (concepts of individual and national rights, political parties, organised protest, trade unions), with the vocabulary and metaphors of contention being those which had served European protestors for decades, even as long as a century.

The intense Ho, quickly involved in international revolutionary activity when he was one of the delegates who supported the position of Moscow and Lenin at the 1920 French Socialist Party convention at Tours, was exceptional, if not unique. First commanding attention by a list of colonial grievances he drew up and submitted to the various delegations at the Paris Peace Conference, Ho then wrote for the Communist newspaper, *L'Humanité*, travelled to the Soviet Union in 1924 and then, in 1925, established, while in China, the Vietnamese Young League of Revolutionaries. In all of this, Ho held on to the notion that doctrine and action must be combined. In this sense, his early efforts were both elitist and intellectual. Yet, although far to the Left in his opinions, he centred his activities on two principal objectives which were really nationalistic: 'to over-throw French imperialism' and its supporting elements; to 'make Indochina completely independent'. For 40 years he devoted himself to achieving both and eventually did. The Saigon of the old order was renamed Ho Chi Minh City in the new, the one that emerged after both the French and the Americans had been forced from the country.

In another part of the colonial world, where also there was an awakening to the inequity of the French administration and, con-comitantly, a demand for change, the response was somewhat different, more cooperative than confrontational in mood. Next to Indochina, North Africa was the French dominated region that was most politically alert, most unsettling to the colonial administration. In Tunisia, Habib Bourguiba, an ambitious young lawyer and journalist, who would later be president of the republic, formed the Neo-Destour Party shortly after the date of Ho's announced objec-tives, in 1934, but with two entirely different immediate objectives: dialogue and mediation. In his now famous phrase, Bourguiba stated that the Neo-Destour Party had to become 'the only true spokesman (*interlocuteur valable*), the authentic representative of Tunisian Tunisia'. For Bourguiba the French presence was of such current strength that other attitudes would have been futile.[4]

Unlike Indochina, where militant activity was very disturbing to the French, the colonial authorities were chiefly confronted with reformist movements in North Africa of the interwar period. These groups reached into the local past for popular support and gained strength by holding out a future of fundamental colonial change, if not disappearance. The Destour Party, for instance, the party that preceded Bourguiba's in influence in Tunisia, had chosen its name – Destour means 'Constitution' – from the Tunisian Constitution of 1861 which had been forced from the Bey through local upheaval and which provided the rudiments of parliamentary government. What the Destour Party wanted in the 1920s was closer French alignment to the concept of the protectorate, the allowance of greater local autonomy in government.

In Morocco and Algeria, where religious interests were stronger than in Tunisia, reformists turned to traditional Islam, sought the purification of institutions and practices allowed to decay and upheld the Islamic past against the Western secular present. The Association of Reformist Ulamas established religious schools which in the 1930s were teaching youngsters a catechism with obvious political implications: 'Islam is my religion, Arabic is my language, Algeria is my fatherland'. In Morocco, the influence of what has been called the 'Arab Awakening' was popular. There the fundamentalist movement called 'Salafiyya' sought a return to the older, the purer Islam, just as the French were making their occupation of Morocco effective. How influential such religious fundamentalism was in the development of modern nationalism there is highly debatable, but the movement did disturb the French and did arouse Moroccans to a new awareness of their own cultural heritage.

THE LITERATURE OF COLONIAL PROTEST

If there is a date that might mark the appearance of a serious literature of colonial protest that was attended with equal seriousness in France, it would be 1921, the year that the novel *Batouala* won the coveted Goncourt Prize. Written by a Martiniquan, Paul Maran, who had served in the French colonial administration in Africa, and described by its author as a 'true Negro novel', *Batouala* generated controversy among the prize selection committee and yet became an immediate success. The divided vote of that committee – five-to-five – was broken in Maran's favour by the president of the Goncourt Academy. Yet, according to the *Literary Digest* of 4 February 1922:

> So quickly did the news of the award spread in Paris that ten minutes after the decision had been announced, a book-buyer, hurrying to the nearest store, found six people ahead of him – all vociferously demanding copies of *Batouala*![5]

The narrative of the novel was laced with bitter commentary about the colonial situation but was not unreservedly favourable to African conditions and culture. The hero of the novel, an African named Batouala, through whom the story is chiefly told, remarks of the French, 'Until my last breath, I will reproach them for their cruelty, their duplicity, their greed'. However, the most telling and quoted comment, epigrammatic in quality, is found not in the narrative, but in the preface, and it concerns the well-known French metaphor, the 'torch of civilization' (think only of the late nineteenth-century symbolic French gift to the United States: the

Statue of Liberty). 'You are not a torch,' Maran writes of the French, 'but a fire. Whatever you touch, you consume.'

Now badly dated by the fast course of events over the 70 years that have passed since its publication, the novel was deemed radical and controversial in its time. Not only was it the first major work of fiction written in French by a black author, but it also was the first such novel attempting to capture the mood and the language of someone looking at the colonial situation from the inside out, from the perspective of a black African. As the anonymous commentator who reviewed the book in *The Literary Digest* remarked, the elements of the novel come together to 'make a tale so strange, so powerful, and so unusual that there is no difficulty in seeing why the ten members of the Académie Goncourt awarded it their prize'.[6]

Maran had attempted to describe Africa for an audience that was only then, in the interwar period, expressing an interest in what would later be termed Afro-American culture. In Paris, where *Batouala* was so excitingly greeted, cultural diversity was in fashion. In the cabarets, one could hear blues music and calypso; on the stage one could see what were called 'Negro Revues', but more compelling was the singular success of the American black singer and dancer Josephine Baker who even rivalled in popularity the great French cabaret singer, Mistinguett. In the museums one could examine African art; and in the bookshops, one could find a variety of studies on the peoples and conditions of the colonial world, with the pace-setting, if hardly the most carefully edited, work being the *Anthologie nègre*, composed by the poet and journalist, Blaise Cendrars, and published in 1921 with an English edition entitled *African Saga* appearing in 1927. Along with these cultural events of appeal primarily to a French audience, there was a flourishing of 'little magazines', giving expression to a new colonial literature written and edited by colonial students then in Paris, of whom the one to become most famous was Léopold Sédar Senghor, later an eminent poet and first president of the Republic of Senegal.

It was in this new cultural climate that Maran's novel appeared, a work that he insisted 'was completely objective', an explanation of the way things were, life was lived. His Africans, he stated, 'suffered and laughed at their suffrance'. Theirs was a different but noble culture, one that was misunderstood and hence mistreated by the French.

To the French argument that the need for international well-being and local modernisation – the variant of the 'dual mandate' – were the reasons for France's assumed responsibility to impose cultural change, certain authors like Maran made the retort that such an imagined responsibility was in fact a form of cultural oppression. In the guise of reform, the colonial powers were depriving the colonial peoples of their own right to retain and develop their own culture according to their own desires and needs.

In these expressions of concern for what anthropologists were now describing as the study of comparative cultures, the most interesting development of the time was the manner in which the pastoral myth was restructured to stand against the urban-industrial one. The comparison frequently made between the two was a moral one, perhaps *moral*, for the French connotation of the adjective includes mores and customs, a way of doing things.

With the war experience standing as refutation of the notion that technological progress would assure human betterment, with the Depression experience serving as an agonising reminder that material goods did not always properly clothe the good, with the pace and intensity of urban life now ulcerating rather than liberating, the Western mind was open to some self-doubt and thereby turned to show some interest in other cultures with different prevailing principles. And so were the minds of writers in the colonial world who were seeking a new voice as well as a new expression.

It was *négritude*, a special celebration of the antithesis of Western civilisation, that was the most unusual colonial literary movement of the time. *Négritude* was not a major factor in the early phase of decolonisation, but it stands – beyond standing in its own right as a major element in modern African literature – as one of the best expressions of disaffection with those Western values that were constantly mentioned as justifications for colonial rule.[7]

First expressed by a youthful group of Haitians who called themselves the *Griots*, or troubadours, offered as a cultural protest against the occupation of that island by the American Marines in 1915 and against the modern educational policy the occupation administration intended to impose, *négritude* was the name given to this assertion of the dignity and value of black culture.

Négritude as a literary movement gained definition in Paris where blacks from the Caribbean and from Africa met with American blacks like Langston Hughes, to discuss their heritage and to give it

expression in essay and poem. It complemented the soon well-
known epigram, 'Black is beautiful', coined by the Jamaican Marcus
Garvey. *Négritude* was not a literary effort to rehabilitate old values
and institutions but to bring their beauty and significance to
Western attention – and to the attention of the young black
intellectuals themselves. It was an affirmation of the contribution
that African-based culture could, should make to a world dominated
by Western geometric patterns. Léopold Sédar Senghor described
the difference between the two cultural patterns – and the complementary value of the African – in his famous poem, 'New York',
composed in 1946 but representative of sentiments formed much
earlier:

> New York, I say to you: New York let black
>   blood flow into your blood
> That it may rub rust from your steel joints,
>   like an oil of life,
> That it may give to your bridges the bend of
>   buttocks and the suppleness of creepers.[8]

The natural curves by which Senghor defines African life will
soften the hard edges of industrial modernity. It is the rhythm of
the pastoral – the beat of the tom-tom or the thump of pestle in
mortar as grain is ground – that he rejoices in. And so does Aimé
Césaire, poet, anti-colonialist, later deputy from Martinique, and
the individual who coined the term *négritude*. Césaire is best
remembered in African literature for *Return to My Native Land*, first
published in 1939, a work which has many of the qualities of an
epic. A long poem of the voyage of self-discovery, it describes
Césaire's return to Martinique after years of study in France. It is
a return to his individuality defined by place, penetrated by
environment, at one with where it is, where it must be:

> My Négritude is neither a tower nor a cathedral
>   it thrusts into the red flesh of the soil
>   it thrusts into the warm flesh of the sky
>   it digs under the opaque dejection of its
>   rightful patience
> *Eia* for the royal *Kailcedrat*!
> *Eia* for those who invented nothing

> *Eia* for those who have never discovered
> for those who have never conquered
> but, struck, deliver themselves to the essence
> of all things.[9]

These lines clearly reveal the two basic elements of *négritude*: the pastoral myth and the existentialist mood. Both stood in contradiction to the rational analysis that was the method of measurement of modern imperialism. The order of the *pax colonia* implied the disorder of the world upon which it was imposed. 'Reason, I crown you the wind of the night,' Césaire declared in his poem. 'Your name, the voice of order?/It becomes the whip's corolla.'[10]

DISHARMONY IN THE 'PAIX FRANÇAISE'

Beyond the familiar punctuation marks for question and surprise, there were stronger signs of dissent. The *paix française* was tremulous at best. Requests for reform still prevailed over calls for revolution, but the tenseness of urgency was for the first time felt in many places.

By its very presence, colonial rule implied social and cultural transition. New customs and a foreign language disturbed old folkways; a wage economy turned to profit dislodged the older self-sufficiency and family labour practices of the countryside. French concepts of private property, when joined with the 'right of conquest', altered land patterns, intensifying large landholdings and allowing the establishment of a rural bourgeoisie composed both of French colonists and those few among the indigenous population who became collaborators in the colonial enterprise. In the rich 'rice bowl' of Vietnam, for instance, about 1000 families out of a global number of 250 000 with property of 50 hectares or more owned 45% of the land.[11] In another continent, the French who had established a protectorate over Tunisia in 1881 had laid their hands on about one million hectares of the richest land by the end of World War I.

The converse of this concentration of wealth was impoverisation of large numbers of the colonial peoples. Removed from traditional modes of farming or grazing, primarily through land expropriation, they were reduced to sharecropping or forced into becoming part of a non-urban proletariat, as were the rubber plantation and coal-mine workers in Vietnam, jointly numbering over 200 000 by 1930.

Equally important, which is to say disruptive, was the locus of modernity, the colonial city. In the interwar period, it was a place of newspapers, of street cars, of shanty towns, of schools and of meetings of small groups of literati. The colonial city was the place where an urban proletariat was growing, called primarily to the functions of the port, not the factory, but underpaid, overworked, ill-considered. The colonial city was the place of a growing consciousness of the grave disparities in the colonial system and of a new historical consciousness of what was there before the French had intruded.

Just as many individuals in the colonial population had mastered the mechanics of driving a motor car by this time, so many others put to use the political devices by which the modern European nation state had been fashioned. The political party, the political rally, the strike and the riot – here were instruments that could effect change, perhaps nearly as easily as they could change hands. In simple terms colonial protest was in colonial terms: words, ideologies, institutions imported. Whether the intended objective was to modify or to destroy colonial rule, the general purpose was dissent of a modern sort.

Yet the process was not unidirectional, a straight line from Paris to Hanoi or Tunis. The colonial phenomenon was international. Protest against it, as would later be the dismantling of its parts, was also international. The activities of the Koumintang in China directly influenced the shape and substance of Vietnamese nationalism; the activities of Mustapha Kemal and his constitutional movement in Turkey after the collapse of the Ottoman Empire directly influenced French North African political developments. The thought and poetry of American blacks, during the flourishing of the Harlem Renaissance in the 1920s, affected the concepts and moods of *négritude*, as has already been stated above. And, most obviously, the outward thrust of the Third Communist International, the 'Comintern', had noticeable effects: both the Vietnamese Communist Party and the *Etoile Nord Africaine*, an Algerian revolutionary party, had their origins and found much of their doctrine in the Communist nest.

In scale, if not in substance, the colonial and anti-colonial forces were balanced: both were internationalised in the interwar period.

All activities remained local in their particulars; all were affected by global conditions in their essentials.

None was more obvious, perhaps more generative of change than the one no one rejoiced over: World War I and its effects. This war, as critics have said since the moment its guns were silenced, changed the disposition of world power: all the European colonial empires were weakened by it, and yet, ironically, now found new strength in the colonies.

For France, the colonies in wartime primarily meant needed manpower. Well before the war, an argument had been made – notably by Lieutenant-Colonel Charles Mangin in a popularly acclaimed study – that Black Africa would be a military 'reservoir' from which a demographically impaired France, its birth rate having fallen below that of all European nations except Ireland, and thus with smaller numbers of young men as potential soldiers than were found in Germany, could draw.[12] Africa was not to be alone in this service. Before the war was over, some 800 000 men had been recruited from the colonial empire: 600 000 combatants and 200 000 workers.

These figures translate into important social developments. First, the local economies and administrations were dislocated by the war. In Senegal, for instance, peanut production, all the more important during the war as French agricultural production slumped, was hindered by the movement of farmers from the local scene to the Western Front. Moreover, military recruitment was in many instances out-and-out impressment with the indigenous populations forced to give up their own youth and with the occasional result of resistance, as in West Africa in 1916–17, where the French encountered revolts in Niger, the Ivory Coast, Dahomey and the Sudan.

By 1917 the desperate French manpower shortage led Georges Clemenceau, both premier and war minister, to develop a bold plan. He asked Blaise Diagne, the first black African deputy elected to the French parliament, to head a recruitment mission to West Africa and offered him the power and authority which would rank him with the governor-general of the territory, a decision without precedent anywhere in the colonial world. Hesitant at first, Diagne accepted the assignment and fulfilled his obligation bountifully. He raised 60 000 instead of the requested 40 000 men. But he did so for good reason. France was to pay for 'this blood price' in the form of citizenship, pensions and some job opportunities given to the African veterans.[13]

While their services were extolled by the French in a number of books and articles that appeared immediately after the war, the colonial troops were seen as exploited by other authors, critics from the colonies themselves. Léon Damas in his concluding poem in a collection entitled *Pigments*, published in 1939, found the war effort misdirected, urged all past and future Senegalese soldiers 'to begin by invading Senegal', to fight against, not with the French. Ho Chi Minh assessed the contribution of the indigenous soldiers to the war effort in a cynical tone. In his collection of essays published in 1925, *Procès de la colonisation* ('Colonialism on Trial'), he remarked, in the chapter entitled 'A Blood Tax', that the soldiers who died in the mud of the Marne and of Champagne, 'allowed themselves to be heroically massacred so that their blood would water the laurels of the military leaders and so that their bones would be sculpted into the batons of marshals'.[14]

There is no way to measure the influence of the war on colonial developments, other than to assert its importance. It awakened more people in the colonies to the disparity between French deeds and words, between the real burden and imagined benefits of empire. It created the international dimensions of the colonial problem, measured by the collapse of old empires like that of Turkey and the appearance of new states, of which the Soviet Union was the most intrusive in colonial affairs.

In that period between the two world wars which drastically altered world conditions to the great disadvantage of the European overseas empires, the colonial situation became less certain. In no area of activity was this more evident than in politics.

The units of the French empire were political entities first and foremost. Political protest was therefore the most widespread and energetic form of dissent. The political party was a new institution, but one that spread widely in the interwar period. The leaders of the Tunisian Neo-Destour Party had, according to Hedi Nouira, one of its members commenting in 1954 on its interwar origins, 'borrowed their tactics, their organization, and their slogans from French political parties'. In some instances, the French party was shipped overseas. The Socialist Party appeared in North Africa before the war, and it was introduced to West Africa by Blaise Diagne in the 1920s. After the party split at Tours in 1920, Communist sections also appeared in North Africa, but were predominantly of French membership. As has been mentioned, the most revolutionary and anti-colonial was the Indochinese Communist Party founded in 1930.

In registering these parties on any historical scale designed to measure degrees of decolonisation, there is the danger of imparting to them more significance – authority, popularity, definition – than in fact they had at the time. Only after World War II does the term 'mass party' have widespread validity. What was generally witnessed in the interwar period is that special form of organisation frequently called by political scientists a 'patron' or 'cadre' party, the first term perhaps the better because it implies the important role of individual leadership.

The cellular quality of the colonial political party is another characteristic. Compact, still isolated from the main body of political and administrative activity, the party may have numbered a few hundred or a few thousand ardent supporters (the Indochinese Communist Party, for instance, had 7 founding members and a total of less than 3000 in the later 1930s) but lacked that major Western quality: a supportive electorate. The simple truth is the mass party depends on the individual vote. Universal suffrage in French colonial territory is a late phenomenon, only realised in the very last years of imperial control. In the early 1920s, for instance, only 421 000 Algerians, out of a population of some 8 000 000, had the right to vote and this in a filtered political system of 'two colleges' with the important powers reserved to the first or French-dominated electoral college.

Universal suffrage was a condition inconsistent with the nature of colonial rule, rule assured by the unqualified strength of the colonial power. 'French sovereignty' was the key issue, expressed in the inherent colonial dilemma: how to allow, even encourage political development without sacrificing control. Even Delavignette's new formula, *humanisme et commandement*, did not provide so much as a pleasing verbal balance.

On the other side, those chaffing under French colonial rule were organising to gain control. No one made a greater effort at this and no one better knew how to negotiate and manipulate to advantage than did Ho Chi Minh. He was well placed, centred in the most troubled of the French possessions, the one in which the French had a tenuous hold. A French creation, an administrative convenience, Indochina was a federation which violated old political boundaries, as well as the mandarin system of administration. The federation was initially characterised by its bureaucratisation, with Frenchmen occupying almost all of the new positions and with the number of positions exceeding that which the Vietnamese had found satisfactory for centuries. Finally, in their determination to make Indochina economically attractive to capitalists and economically beneficial to France, the administration launched an ambitious programme of rail and road building, of encouragement of new export industries of which rubber was the most famous. These economic activities brutally harnessed Vietnamese labour.

In this culturally disrupted environment, Vietnamese gathered in protest. They rioted, as in a famous riot of 1907 against taxes, or in a series of upheavals that occurred during World War I when the French were hard-pressed to maintain order. These discontented persons acquired that personal state in many ways: they wrote; they travelled, notably to Japan; they studied. They also gathered in France, where it was officially estimated some 1556 had concentrated in 1930. It was from among this group that the first major colonial student protest took place before the presidential residence, the Elysée Palace, when over one hundred Vietnamese students and workers gathered in complaint against the death sentence meted out to participants in the Yen Bey abortive coup.

Yen Bey occupies an important place in the political history of decolonisation. It was a failure, but it strongly demonstrated the degree of discontent with French rule. In Vietnam, more than elsewhere at this time, a combination of growing intellectual ferment, French censorship and closing of publications considered radical, economic discontent aggravated by the world depression, and the authoritarian nature of French rule led to seething discontent. Although there were several political groups organising in protest, the one that became immediately most important was the Viet Nam Quoc Dan Dang, the Vietnam National Party, the VNQDD, organised in Hanoi in December of 1927. Through alliances, the party grew in size and significance but soon suffered a loss of leadership as the result of the murder of a Frenchman in 1929, an act attributed to the VNQDD and precipitating the French arrest, jailing or executing of the party leadership. Those who escaped this political fate moved toward drastic action. In 1930, a decision was reached to attack French military posts in the North, those located around the Red River delta so as 'to destroy French colonial authority', in the words of the plotters.[15]

The plan was poorly executed on the night of 9–10 February 1930, but with the strongest thrust made against the garrison of Yen Bey. The hoped for support from Vietnamese in the French colonial army at that base did not occur; the revolt was quickly and brutally put down. The VNQDD was a victim of its own actions. A nationalist party, with strong support among the emerging middle classes, its failure at Yen Bey cleared the way for the success and predominance of the Indochinese Communist Party, unified from several divergent elements on 3 February 1930.

In large measure that achievement was the work of Ho Chi Minh who early on connected Communism and anticolonialism when he read Lenin's 'Theses on the National and Colonial Questions'. Stating in an article that he wrote for a Soviet publication in 1925 that 'Lenin was the first to realize and assess the full importance of drawing the colonial peoples into the revolutionary movement', Ho subscribed to Communist theory but acted as a realistic nationalist.[16] Thus, he first organised the League of Vietnamese Revolutionary Youth in Canton, China, to arouse spirited anticolonialism, a sense of national purpose, and to acquaint its members with Marxist–Leninist thought. The League was rather short-lived, its membership fragmenting as efforts were made to set up a Communist party in part to respond with leadership to the increasing popular strikes that were then occurring in Vietnam. Ho was out of Vietnam at the time but summoned representatives of the disjointed groups to Hong Kong where he organised the new party and resolved the pressing issue of its name. On 3 February 1930, the Communist Party of Vietnam was formed.

Its initial fortunes were not, however, propitious. Shortly after the failure of Yen Bey, soviets, peasant councils and cells, appeared in the northern area known as Nghe Tinth as a political reaction to the harsh economic conditions of the time. The seizure of estates, marches against the government and strikes placed the colonial authority in a condition of disarray. With a limited number of French troops available, but with the support of French Legionnaires in the colony, the government proceeded slowly to react in the autumn of 1930. By the end of the year, the upheaval, the most significant in French interwar colonial history, had abated as a result of French military pressure and declining enthusiasm among the local population. Then, the new Communist Party leadership was broken up, some members arrested and others fleeing. A certain calm fell over Indochina, more a calm of exhaustion and anticipation than of security. The potential of popular upheaval had been demonstrated.

As for Ho Chi Minh, his next few years remain a mystery. In Hong Kong at the time of the arrests, he was to be extradited by the British to the French in Indochina. Official reports of the time state that he died of tuberculosis, his body like his name supposedly wasting away. In 1941 when he again appeared as a name and a personality, the French colonial authorities registered disbelief. In 1945 when the French returned to Indochina after the disasters of World War II, the French were not surprised to encounter resistance. Ho had returned before them.

THE COLONIAL SITUATION ON THE EVE OF WORLD WAR II

Disbelief in the continuation of colonial rule was not yet widespread among French colonial authorities or politicians at home. They read the signs of protest as limited, just as they read the expressions of support as genuine. Indeed, many of the colonised, certainly among those who were well-educated, were comfortable with the colonial situation, by which they profited as businessmen, as lawyers, even a few as doctors. Among this same group there were some who looked with hope on the French efforts and therefore anticipated that appropriate action, particularly assistance with the modernisation of old cultures, would follow the generous language of French ideology.

There were others who assumed that their political future was allied with that of France. In 1936, Ferhat Abbas, one of the most vocal of those Algerians calling for reform, issued what has become a classic statement. In an article for the publication *L'Entente*, he wrote: 'If I had found the Algerian nation, I would have been a nationalist'. But his questioning of the living and the dead in Algeria, of culture present and culture past, he continued, only revealed a series of imperial pasts, Arab and Muslim empires now gone. Pushing aside what he described as nationalist 'clouds and dreams', he declared that Algerians had 'to join their future to the French endeavors in this country'.[17] In 1945, Léopold Sédar Senghor expressed his hope for a 'French Imperial Community'.[18]

The French were not yet ready to contemplate either autonomy or independence as a serious alternative to colonial rule. Most of the newly arising colonial leaders could not yet foresee a future in which they would be chiefs of state rather than collaborators with the French.

When World War II broke out, the French devised a political poster prominently displaying the British and French empires in red – while that of Nazi Germany appeared in black – on a map of the world. 'We will win because we are bigger than they are,' the poster announced with determination. For a brief moment, on a propaganda poster, the French had a clear view of their colonial empire as an entity and as a force. That view was quickly lost, as was so much else, in the thick clouds generated by the war.

4 The Despair and Hope of War

German newsreels of June 1940 mockingly showed black African troops as prisoners of war. France's colonial manpower, mustered in 1939 as it had been in 1914, availed little in preventing a stunning defeat which hastily removed France from the ranks of the great powers. In the political debris of that bleak summer, only the overseas empire held any promise for France in world affairs. The significance of that empire was dramatically highlighted even as the Germans overran France and the French sought an armistice. Several members of the French government, temporarily relocated in the city of Bordeaux, considered setting up a new seat of power in North Africa to continue the war from that location. They set sail from Bordeaux to Casablanca on the French cruiser *Massilia*, arrived on June 24, with the energetic minister of defence, Georges Mandel, issuing a proclamation of government with himself as premier. He was quickly detained and arrested, the episode a minor one in the war but one symbolic of the new dependence that a shattered France had assumed toward its colonial empire.

For the armistice government, installed after the peace agreement signed with the Germans on June 22 and then settled in the spa city of Vichy, the empire was a potentially important element in a policy of meaningful collaboration with the New Order which at the time gave the appearance of permanence as German troops occupied two-thirds of France and the German war machine threatened to crush Great Britain with its airpower. For the self-styled Free French, determined to carry on the war and temporarily refuged in England, the convictions of General Charles de Gaulle were the invisible bond that joined the little group of 7000 men into a force of national liberation. For de Gaulle, in that first summer of exile, the colonial empire was the promise of a revived France, a France once again to be ranked among the great powers. De Gaulle so argued later in the first volume of his war memoirs:

49

In the vast spaces of Africa France could in fact rebuild its armies and reacquire its sovereignty, while awaiting the alignment of new allies along with the old to change the military balance.[1]

AN EMPIRE DIVIDED

However, in that eventful summer of 1940 what was most significant to any global observer was the competing French efforts to assure colonial authority, as Vichy struggled to hold on and as de Gaulle struggled to wrest away. The divided French fought over the French empire.

The first violent encounter was an early naval engagement which occurred at Dakar on 23–24 September 1940. General de Gaulle, in his later interpretation of that impending encounter, provided a dramatic reading:

At sea, in the blackness of night, on the swell of a heaving ocean, a pathetic foreign ship, without guns, with all lights extinguished, carried the destiny of France.[2]

That destiny consisted of de Gaulle himself and the small invasion force he had mustered with British help, and which included Dutch ships, on one of which de Gaulle sailed.

Already assured of support from most of French Equatorial Africa, a region far south of Senegal, de Gaulle now hoped to inspire the French West African Federation to join him by a show of force before its capital port. Instead he encountered severe resistance which had been hastily reinforced by French naval units that had left Toulon and slipped past the British at Gibraltar. The joint Anglo-French expedition had little choice but to withdraw from Dakar, the chief effect of the operation being the impression it left on the minds of men far from the scene. The Vichy government used the incident to convince the Germans of unquestioned loyalty; Winston Churchill and Franklin D. Roosevelt were deeply disappointed in the failure of the undertaking and accordingly were sceptical of further joint ventures with de Gaulle.[3]

Failure at Dakar only accentuated the divided nature of the French colonial empire. All of North Africa and West Africa, as well as Indochina, remained loyal to Vichy, while more outlying and less consequential regions like New Caledonia and Equatorial Africa stood beside the general. De Gaulle, in the second volume of his memoirs, asserts the global importance of the support he immediately received from French Equatorial Africa. Describing a meeting he had in Cairo in August of 1942 with Jan Smuts, then prime minister of the Union of South Africa, de Gaulle quotes Smuts as saying that if such support had not occurred, then he, Smuts, would have lost control of South Africa with the result that the pro-Axis elements in that country would have pushed for a policy of collaboration with Nazi Germany, thus threatening all of Africa with German hegemony.[4]

Debatable, of course, the analysis offered by Smuts is important because it was included by de Gaulle in his memoirs as proof of his role in the determination of the course of the war even in its early days. However, at the time of the melodramatic and failed attack on Dakar the colonial affairs of Vichy, not of Charles de Gaulle, appeared to be by far the more successful. The reason for this immediate outcome was certainly not the result of military strength, which Vichy completely lacked, but because of a long-established institutional authority which seemed to transcend particular regime, a condition that might be called bureaucratic submission. Pierre Boisson, Delegate-General of Vichy in French West Africa at the time of de Gaulle's naval raid, best described the condition. He feared that disobedience to established authority would weaken colonial rule. 'Movements that do not respect hierarchy carry within themselves the ferment of dissolution,' he solemnly stated to his subordinates.[5] Where allegiance was hesitant, Vichy sent loyal replacements for chief administrators.

In the days immediately after France's defeat when Charles de Gaulle tried to create a power base that would support his rhetorical stand, the Vichy government counted the colonial empire as one of its remaining sources of strength. The other was the French fleet. These two elements of French national power figured large in Mediterranean affairs, an assessment made by the Germans as well as by the British. Furthermore, the Vichy government, notably in the person of its premier, Pierre Laval, saw the empire as a means of establishing a meaningful policy of collaboration with Germany through which Hitler's New Europe would stretch across the Mediterranean.[6]

Underlying such French thought were considerations other than strategy. Old animosities toward Great Britain, most deeply felt by naval personnel, were still held. Defeat might now allow revenge, some officers thought, providing an opportunity to settle old scores with France's traditional colonial and naval rival. This bitter past had been brutally rushed into the present when Winston Churchill, fearing that the numerous units of the French fleet based at Mers-El-Kebir in Algeria might return to France and fall into German hands, ordered action against that fleet. As the British squadron lay off the coast on 3 July 1940, the French commander was given an ultimatum consisting of three choices: to join the British; to remove his ships to another part of the empire, namely Martinique; to scuttle the ships. The refusal of all three alternatives led to immediate British naval engagement: the shelling and sinking of the anchored French fleet, with a high loss of French life.

The Vichy government, particularly its naval officers, were angered and stunned. (General de Gaulle was furious on first learning of the event, but later coldly accepted the fact.) More important in colonial matters, the action deterred the growing colonial support for de Gaulle, caused the number of exiles joining his group in England to dwindle, and intensified the argument for Franco-German collaboration against the British. Thus, Pierre Laval, in a reversal of the late nineteenth-century spirit of French *revanche* ('revenge') against Germany for having seized Alsace and Lorraine at the end of the Franco-Prussian War of 1870, now argued that the current loss of Alsace to the Germans might be compensated by British territory in Africa.

Away from the petty squabbles and awkward relationship with Nazi Germany that marked French domestic politics, the colonial possessions nevertheless suffered from economic disarray, a condition that aggravated discontent. Commerce all but ceased, with shortages of imports compounded by the storage of exports. The colonial economy, never sound and still suffering from the effects of the Depression, was further weakened with the result that the local populations suffered from a loss of income and endured deprivation of certain food stuffs. Lack of maritime movement also meant no replacement of administrative staffs. In Indochina, the Vichy Governor-General, Admiral Jean Decoux, began to employ Anna-mites in bureaucratic positions they had never held before, thus involving the indigenous population in an almost revolutionary administrative way.

More significant was the unexpected international interest that the French colonial empire acquired because several of its territories now stood along the broad avenues of war. Both deprived of sufficient military and naval support to act with a considerable degree of independence and responsible to a government which was itself subservient to another nation, the overseas territories loyal to Vichy were exposed and susceptible to invasion and conquest.

French North Africa was particularly worrisome and inviting. The Germans had considered a sweep through the Mediterranean and into the French possessions as a possible military action immediately after the fall of France. However, Hitler's inability to win over Generalissimo Francesco Franco to military engagement on the Nazi side (even after Hitler had given Franco a handsome Mercedes touring car) effectively ended any further consideration of the proposal. Italy, long in rivalry with France in North Africa, still desired acquisition of Tunisia and coveted the neighbouring Constantine area of Algeria. But in the tangled negotiations between Vichy France and Nazi Germany, the French were allowed the right to protect their North African possessions against possible British assault, and therefore were granted the right to increase military effectives there. In this indirect way, Italian colonial claims were muted.

The unsettled condition of the French colonial empire was also unsettling to both the British and the Americans. On both sides of the Atlantic, the French African possessions posed a threat and offered a promise. President Franklin D. Roosevelt, in a speech made on 15 May 1941, indicated his concern. 'The delivery of the French Colonial Empire to Germany,' he declared, 'would be a menace to the peace and safety of the Western Hemisphere.'[7] It was that empire, as ocean-fronting real estate, which disturbed American strategists, who envisioned impediments to shipping and security if port cities like Casablanca and Dakar serviced German submarines and other naval craft. As late as 1943, Roosevelt was still concerned. He even toyed with the idea of an international trusteeship system for much of the colonial world in which the United States would act 'as policeman for the United Nations at Dakar'.[8]

The British naval view had long followed the famous 'red line' of empire, the shipping routes through the Mediterranean, then through the Suez Canal and on to India and the Far East. German occupancy of French African territory would therefore be a singular threat to Britain's long-established interests and, of course, to any effective management of the war in the Mediterranean. The arrival of Erwin Rommel's Afrika Korps in Libya in early 1941 and its rapid deployment eastward toward Alexandria later justified Britain's anxiety.

The first anniversary of Rommel's appearance on the colonial scene was celebrated with historical irony. On February 15, the very same day that Rommel had landed in North Africa, the great naval port of Singapore, considered impregnable, fell to the Japanese. That Far Eastern military disaster of 1942 was brutal proof of the global nature of this war and the position colonial possessions assumed in it. Southeast Asia had been as worrisome to the French as it had been to the British since the moment that Japanese naval authority had been established in that oceanic region in the early twentieth century. The fall of Port Arthur, after a long naval siege by the Japanese during the Russo-Japanese War of 1904–5, was taken by French authors as a frightening augury of things to come. The sight of the defeated Russians being marched away by the victorious Japanese was not the sight of 'one people defeated by another', wrote the correspondent for the Parisian newspaper *Le Temps*. 'It was something new and earth-shaking: it was the victory of one world over another . . . .'[9] The rise of Japan was, however, viewed from two distinct angles by Frenchmen in the interwar era. There were those who saw Japan as a bulwark against an expanding Communism which was perceived as moving across the Continent from the Soviet Union to China and, so it was feared, on to Indochina in an effort to overthrow French colonial authority. There were others who saw Japan as expansionist, 'inclined to consider itself as the predestined sovereign of the Pacific', according to Georges Hardy.[10] France's role, most concluded, could only be that of interested spectator as the major Pacific powers – Japan, the Soviet Union, Great Britain and the United States – manoeuvred for position.

Even that role was soon denied as the course of the war made the French colonial possessions elements of military strategy in which the French had little part.

THE COURSE OF MILITARY EVENTS IN NORTH AFRICA AND INDOCHINA

After the American entry into the war, North Africa was reassigned on military maps, although not immediately. The political-military debate over possible invasion routes into the Nazi empire is a fascinating, now somewhat amusing tale. Personal preferences, national differences, uncertain assessments of the Soviet ability to continue resistance and of the British ability to withstand Rommel in Libya and Egypt complicated the matter. The list of code names for the various Allied military plans against Germany today makes an interesting little literary history of its own. What remains important in this exercise in metaphor, however, was the decision to delay an invasion of Europe and to proceed with one in North Africa. The North African campaign, remarked the American Secretary of War, Henry Stimson, was President Roosevelt's 'secret war baby'. It was also Churchill's. Upon learning of Roosevelt's agreement to the plan, Churchill 'hastened to rechristen my favorite', he later wrote in his history of the war. The new code name (it had previously been 'Gymnast', 'Super-Gymnast', and 'Semi-Gymnast') for the operation was to be 'Operation Torch'.[11]

French North Africa was thus designated a military theatre, a southern front from which to move against the Continental territory of Nazi Germany. This Churchillian grand vision of military affairs, supported by President Roosevelt, was not one shared by the American chief of staff, General George Marshall, who saw the proposed operation as 'dispersionist' and 'peripheral'. The forthcoming operation was also viewed with disfavour by General de Gaulle because he and the Free French were excluded from any involvement. 'Everything was henceforth clear', he said upon learning of the planned invasion. 'The strategy of the Allies is well determined. As for their political behaviour, it is nothing more than damnable egoism,' he wrote.[12]

Without de Gaulle, the invasion took place on 8 November 1942. Vichy French military resistance in Morocco and Algeria, where the campaign took place, was both confused and minimal, leading to quick Allied success, such that the major objectives of the campaign, the port cities of Casablanca, Algiers and Oran, were all secured within two days. However, the Germans quickly responded by moving into Tunisia from bases they had established in Sicily. Their military strength was sufficient to hold off final Allied success in the North African campaign until February of 1943.

While embittered and negotiating for a role in North Africa, de Gaulle, describing himself as 'determined to be unshakable', proceeded to extend the authority of the Free French over the colonial empire in the Indian ocean, largely through negotiation with the British and in face of the collapse of any Vichy authority in France, now that the Germans had occupied the entire country in response to the North African invasion. In December of 1942, first Réunion, then Madagascar, and, thereafter, French Somaliland rallied to the General.

Events also quickly changed to favour de Gaulle in North Africa. In the confusion of the invasion, Admiral Jean Darlan, then Vichy commander-in-chief of the armed forces, was in Algiers to visit his son, who had suddenly been stricken with infantile paralysis. Darlan's presence gave him, as senior governmental officer, commanding authority. In negotiation with American Brigadier-General Mark Clark, Darlan assumed all authority for the Vichy regime on 10 November and ordered the surrender of French troops on that day. On 24 December 1942, however, Darlan was assassinated, an event that removed considerable political embarrassment for the Allies, but one that also led to cooperation between the French colonial troops in North Africa, which were now placed by the Allies under the command of General Henri Giraud, and the Free French of General de Gaulle. However, the relationship between Giraud and de Gaulle, never good, quickly deteriorated. By the time the National Committee of Liberation had transferred its seat from London to Algiers on 3 July 1944, Giraud's power was waning. He was soon eased out as co-leader with de Gaulle. Thus, de Gaulle successfully won his own North African campaign.[13]

In the Pacific Theatre of War, Indochina also was made part of military strategy, although the territories of the federation were not to figure prominently in the war itself.[14] The Japanese had determined the need to dominate Indochina years before the war, to have it serve as a secured coast for their growing oceanic empire. With the collapse of France in Europe, Japan quickly assumed an effective indirect control of the colonial administration there. The French were helpless to do much, if anything. Confronted with the defeat at home, the governor-general, General Georges Catroux, immediately sought American assistance in the form of a naval demonstration of strength in the Gulf of Tonkin, an effort to deter the Japanese. This was denied him, as was his request to obtain American aircraft from among those ordered by the French government before its military defeat. Receiving nothing, Catroux was forced to give something, that which Japan had already demanded in an ultimatum: establishment of joint control of the northern border through which the Yunnan railroad, a source of supplies to China, ran.

Catroux was quickly removed by the new Vichy government and replaced by Admiral Jean Decoux. Decoux, headstrong and unswervingly supportive of the Vichy regime, proved to be a rather adroit administrator, making the most of a bad situation, but forced to reach an accord, signed on 22 September 1940, which allowed the Japanese to use and guard Indochinese airports and to transport troops across the peninsula on the colonial railways to the warfront in China. The Japanese allowed the French to retain formal sovereignty of the territory but in effect had become masters of the region. This *ad hoc* arrangement caused little outward disturbance as the French continued to function as the colonial authority while the Japanese troops were concentrated in the north and largely unnoticed.

In the Pacific military scheme of things Indochina played a minor role during the war, although it did occupy President Roosevelt's attention. By all accounts, including his own, the president was appalled, perhaps obsessed, by French colonial rule in the region. Discussing French colonialism with his son Elliott, as Elliott later related the matter, President Roosevelt said:

Or take Indo-China. The Japanese control that colony now. Why was it such a cinch for the Japanese to conquer the land? The native Indo-Chinese has been so flagrantly downtrodden that they thought to themselves: Anything must be better than to live under French colonial rule![15]

Roosevelt spoke of trusteeship as a solution to Indochina's political future, particularly after he realised that China would not be strong enough to play the role of overseer there that he had intended. The British, not anxious to support any effort against colonial empire, argued the importance of France's empire to that nation's position in postwar Europe. However, it was the direct occupation of Indochina by the Japanese in March of 1945 that created a compelling argument for some support to be given the colonial effort of the government of Charles de Gaulle.

DE GAULLE'S COLONIAL PLANS

In this war, the French colonial empire proved to be a problem to all, not a particular strength to any, except, perhaps, Charles de Gaulle.

General Charles de Gaulle neither found his task easy nor the world in which he wished to play a big role benign. He never wavered, however. Headstrong in attitude, determined in historical mission, he imagined France to be something more than it actually was. That false perception was emphasised in an amusing anecdote that de Gaulle related with relish in his war memoirs. Leaving Great Britain, where he had received asylum, for Algeria, where he was to establish his provisional government, de Gaulle was received by Anthony Eden, the Foreign Secretary, at the moment of his farewell. De Gaulle recalls the conversation this way:

"Are you aware," said Mr. Eden to me in good humor, "that you have caused us more difficulties than all our allies in Europe?"

"I don't doubt it," I replied, smiling as well. "France is a great power."[16]

To assure that condition, de Gaulle turned his attention to the colonial empire in the last years of the war. This field of action was not one of choice, for de Gaulle clearly understood, even rejoiced in the fact, that France's global authority necessarily depended on the French nation itself. But pending the moment when France would be liberated, he acted effectively on the periphery.

De Gaulle's intentions, however, were seldom complemented by those of his allies. De Gaulle's personal war experience was one of struggling with the frustration, indeed the anger, he frequently sensed as a result of British and American military policy. The lengthy story, colourful in the documented accusations and counter-accusations, had a simple theme: dislike of de Gaulle and hence disinclination to work closely with him. Neither Winston Churchill nor Franklin D. Roosevelt had much tolerance for the man. De Gaulle, in turn, was suspicious of both of them and was angered or affronted by the military activities they conducted in parts of the French colonial empire without his knowledge or participation. The British invasion of Madagascar on 5 May 1942, was one such instance; the North African invasion of 8 November 1942 was another. Moreover, British activities in the Middle East, in France's formerly mandated territories of Syria and Lebanon, were interpreted by de Gaulle as efforts at colonial aggrandisement.

However, de Gaulle's political position changed with the expected result of the North African invasion: the Nazi decision to occupy all of France. Vichy was thereby deprived of all sovereign territory and thus reduced to a meaningless cipher in international affairs. Accordingly, the Free French of de Gaulle moved closer to becoming a government, now establishing a Committee of National Liberation. De Gaulle was then recognised as the rightful caretaker, perhaps even the heir to the French imperial estate and the nation that had formed it.

Establishing himself in Algiers on 30 May 1943, de Gaulle soon turned his attention to the condition of the colonial empire. He called for a special conference to be held in Brazzaville, an appropriate, if not a convenient site. A previous colonial conference had been held there in November 1941 under the presidency of Félix Eboué, Governor of Chad, who had quickly and enthusiastically declared for de Gaulle in August of that year. That conference had proposed consideration of a new 'native policy' for French Equatorial Africa and concluded that the policy of assimilation should be abandoned in favour of encouragement of local cultures.

The second Brazzaville conference was larger in scope and truly historic in its significance.[17] De Gaulle expected as much. He flew to Brazzaville in stages, a progress made, as he later wrote, with 'deliberate solemnity'.[18]

Bold in its intention and ambiguous in its declarations, the Brazzaville Conference was designed in the minds of its sponsors to reassure the continuation of empire. However, it now stands as a major event in historical interpretations of decolonisation. Organised by René Pleven, who had become the Free French commissioner of colonies, the conference was arranged to adjust the French empire to a new world forged during the war and, not incidentally, to dispel doubts about France's ability to govern colonies well.

In this small colonial city, named after one of France's most intrepid colonial officers, were gathered together colonial administrators, members of the provisional consultative assembly, Eboué, Pleven, and, of course, Charles de Gaulle. Yet the gathering was not imperial, but colonial, its membership composed primarily of individuals from Africa, particularly Sub-Saharan Africa. In another sense the conference was also colonial: not a single representative from any indigenous people was present. Eboué, a black of colonial origin, sat upright in his administrative capacity, that of a high-ranking colonial official.

Opening the conference on 30 January 1944, de Gaulle set the tone by arguing, in broad terms, that the war had changed nothing of a fundamental nature in the colonial relationship:

> We believe that the immense events which have upset the world require us not to delay, that the terrible ordeal which was the temporary occupation of France [la Métropole] by the enemy has in no way taken from wartime France its rights and responsibilities. ...[19]

The general nouns implied certain particulars, however. First and most important, the conference denied the possibility of self-government. The denial was couched in the already archaic terms of nineteenth-century colonial theorists

> The purposes of the civilizing efforts accomplished by France in the colonies rule out any idea of autonomy, any possibility of evolution outside the framework of the French empire. ...[20]

However, the old idea was realigned with new realities. A more active role, a more considered position was to be given the colonial peoples in the imperial system. An incipient system of representative government was suggested, with local consultative assemblies and regional assemblies at the territorial level, with both Africans and French included. Even more daring in concept was the suggestion that the colonies should participate in the affairs of the 'French Community', either through a colonial parliament or a federal assembly.

The condition of the colonial peoples, their well-being, was determined for the first time in their own terms. The term 'political personality' was used in contradistinction to centralisation (the old assimilationist objective) to emphasise the importance of local needs and aspirations. The *indigénat*, the special and harsh judicial code for Africans, was to be abolished, and economic development was to be encouraged. Underlying all, at least in principle, was the assertion that the consideration of the needs and aspirations of the local populations must be the first, the fundamental consideration.

The Brazzaville Conference drew up a series of recommendations; it could do no more. Without authority based on representative government, the conferees prepared an agenda that would be submitted to the new government in France, once it had been established.

The effects of the conference's deliberations were felt far from the banks of the Congo River. The interpretation of what had happened was not favourable in Washington, where French colonialism was always at best suspect in intention. Ralph Bunche, later American representative to the United Nations, and at the time a State Department official, offered this overseas summary:

There was no compromise with the basic principle that French Africa belongs solely to France and is an exclusively French affair. There was no recognition that France owed any accountability to the international community in the conduct of her colonial affairs and that the international community had any interest in such affairs.[21]

The ambiguity of the conference's findings allowed the French to rejoice in reform, the Americans to wonder in doubt and the French colonial peoples to protest in anger or anticipate with hope. Brazzaville was indeed a turning point; the immediate question was: in which direction?

THE COLONIAL SITUATION AT THE END OF THE WAR

The chaos of the war, however, seemed clearly to be amassing in the favour of decolonisation. For all his energy and despite the fulsomeness of his rhetoric, Charles de Gaulle could not give reality to his assertion that France's redemption as a great power would be by way of the nation's colonies. The authority and the initiative which the empire had allowed France were being transferred, away from France. If this development was not yet electrical, as quick and obvious as a reversal of current, it was fluid as is the sea when a vessel's structure shudders and forward progress is slowed with the reversal of the ship's engines.

The French imperial structure briefly shook and then seemed to right itself, to continue its course somewhat longer. But that previous forward motion, the continuation as a French organised and French directed enterprise, stopped. The future direction of the empire was uncertain. However, it was certain that this large and ill-constructed vessel would never return triumphantly to home port.

World War II, in which the Vichy government was isolated and helpless in Nazi-dominated Europe and in which de Gaulle's Free French were abroad with very limited resources, had the effect of compromising empire, in the final analysis everywhere dependent on the power and authority of the national state which formally controlled it. 'Might makes right' was a tired expression in those years and certainly one that the French could not declaim openly, even if they still thought that the clause had meaning.

As the newer imperialism of Nazi Germany and Imperial Japan began its retreat, it carried along with it the old imperialism as well. The briefly imposed new domination where it had occurred abroad and the general disintegration of French political power throughout the world gravely weakened the old imperial authority. Concession and demand were the two attitudes that characterised the colonial situation in the turbulent years of the war.

Syria and Lebanon, mandated to France by the League of Nations but treated as if integral parts of the colonial empire, were told in June 1941 by General Catroux, the Free French representative in that region, that they would henceforth be 'sovereign independent peoples'. This statement was made soon after the Anglo-French military occupation of the territories.

A little over a year later, beginning on 8 November 1942, the Allied invasion of North Africa took place bringing with it the further deterioration of the French colonial position. Achieved primarily by the Americans, brazen in their anti-colonialism and bountiful in their equipment – two factors which did not enhance local respect for the French – the invasion aroused hope among the North Africans and, with it, new demands for colonial reform. Two documents stand out in particular. The first was the letter that accompanied the manifesto of the Istiqlal (Independence) Party of

Morocco, issued on 11 January 1944, and calling for the end of the protectorate and, consequently, for the independence of the country. In the accompanying letter, which the party leadership asked the resident-general to forward to General de Gaulle, the authors stated:

> We think the time has come for France to recognize the blood that Moroccans have shed and will continue to shed if necessary for [France's] ideals and for its own freedom.[22]

In a very similar mood, Algerian Muslim political activists, led by Ferhat Abbas, had requested to meet with the French authorities shortly after the Allied landing in Algeria on 8 November 1942. Their request being ignored, Ferhat Abbas thereupon drew up his now famous 'Manifesto of the Algerian People', which listed as its first demand 'the condemnation and abolition of colonization'.[23] The next two demands followed logically: self-government and a constitution allowing for immediate participation by Algerians in their own political affairs. These latter two demands were made with reference to General Catroux's promises for Syria, a clear suggestion of the wartime cause-and-effect in colonial affairs. The Gaullist provisional government, however, ignored the Manifesto and proceeded at its own pace and in its own way to liberalise the electoral process in Algeria, not to reform it.

The French, despite if not because of their wartime experience, saw no need to change the fundamental basis of colonial empire. René Pleven had asserted in his speech at the Brazzaville Conference that 'there are no peoples to liberate' in the French empire. The colonial peoples, he continued, 'do not want to know any other independence than the independence of France'.[24]

Even before this incredible statement, General de Gaulle had made his own response both in broad terms about the future of the colonial empire and in more particular ones to the Algerian 'Manifesto'. On 12 December 1943, he announced in Algiers his intention to re-establish French authority in Indochina. That news provoked a Vietnam publication entitled *Franco-Nipponese Fascists* which contained this bitter invective: 'So the French, themselves struggling against German domination, hope to maintain their domination over other peoples!'

The French did, and they made the effort to do so. As the war concluded, their chances seemed somewhat brighter. De Gaulle celebrated 14 July 1944, Bastille Day, in Algeria, where he was well-received. Within the year, the French made a few efforts at reform. The electoral system in Algeria was revised to increase substantially the number of Muslim voters, and the 'French Union' was established, bringing together the various colonial territories and promising that 'At the heart of this Union, Indochina will enjoy its own freedom'. Furthermore, talk of federation intensified in the last year of the war, talk that suggested the possibility of a more supple system of rule, with greater respect for regional differences. De Gaulle, in a Washington press conference held on 10 July 1944, said:

> I believe that each territory under the French flag must be represented within a system of a federal kind of which the metropolis shall be a part and where the interests of each individual shall be heard.[25]

What was soon heard was the outcry of discontent and the sound of weapons which supported it.

Then, in those early months of victory, Charles de Gaulle began thinking seriously of the role France might play in Europe. Addressing a convocation of the University of Brussels where he received an honorary degree in October 1945, he expressed his idea for a new Europe of associated states. In this new Europe, he expected France to play the leading role. To do so, retention of the colonial empire was necessary. If France's territorial possessions still remained 'associated' with the nation, he wrote in the last volume of his war memoirs, 'the way will be open for our action on the Continent. Secular destiny of France!' However he knowingly concluded that it would be foolish to assume that the colonial empire could continue as before in the light of the war experience endured on African and Asian soil.

Neither the reforms that Charles de Gaulle had in mind nor those generated by his political successors would alter what had become a definite international trend. The colonies fell apart, were torn away, were hastily abandoned, or were even graciously given up. Such actions occurred everywhere, in the territories of Great Britain, of the Netherlands, as well as those of France. General de Gaulle would anguish personally over this set of developments because the last acts of colonial divestment occurred when he again was president of the French Republic, the Fifth Republic which itself was born in colonial anguish.

5 Caution and Confusion

In his personal account of service in the French Army in Algeria, *Lieutenant in Algeria*, the well-known French publisher Jean-Jacques Servan-Schreiber describes a scene that in retrospect assumes the quality of metaphor. It concerns but one small ground action undertaken by the French.

As the ground troops are deployed in an effort to seek out the Algerian guerrilla force before them, a helicopter carrying the commanding general from Algiers to the scene hovers overhead, and the general, bearing the code name 'Big Soup', inquires, from about 330 feet above, the nature of the operation. Intruding with radioed suggestions, 'Big Soup' annoys the soldiers below, then leaves the scene, but not before he has commended the men and requested from their commanding officer a list of all those who should be recommended for decoration.[1]

That distance assumed by the helicopter-borne general which allowed of a certain abstraction, perhaps even idealisation, of the harsh reality defined below was similar to the perspective on colonial affairs from which French politicians determined the form of the debate and the policy concerning empire after World War II. The need for fundamental reform did not seem near enough to create a sense of urgency, and the reality of change in the world at large was often seen as far away from immediate French concerns. Furthermore, unfamiliarity with the colonial terrain and with the problems and issues that sprang from it allowed for a premature conclusion in no way any different from that radioed by General 'Big Soup' to the troops on the ground: 'All our objectives have been attained'.

HESITANT POLICIES AND TENTATIVE REFORMS

A new vision of the overseas territories was never found. Old methods and old ideas, supported by politicians and colonial administrators who had long been in service, continued. The various

65

changes in the official nomenclature by which the institutions of the overseas territories were described changed little; in fact little changed in the attitudes and activities of those charged with the administration of it all. 'Empire' was no longer found in the political vocabulary, but its replacements, first 'French Union' and then 'Community' served better as rhetorical devices than as descriptions of institutional change.

The persistence of old thought and long-established patterns of behaviour does not, however, allow any simple conclusion that reiterates the old line, *Plus ça change, plus c'est la même chose.* The French were as aware of the new turn of events as were any people, but the one concept and condition with which political leaders did not wish to part was that of sovereignty. Fundamental change necessitated the transfer, not just the adjustment, of political authority from Parisian ministries and territorial governors' palaces to representatives of the indigenous peoples. During the debate over the new constitution for the Fourth Republic, this issue was sufficiently volatile to cause the then Minister of Overseas Territories, Marius Moutet, to declare that he would allow nothing to threaten French sovereignty abroad.[2] His words echoed those of Charles de Gaulle, offered in a discussion of Indochina while he was in Washington, D.C., in 1945. 'For us,' he said, 'this sovereignty is a capital matter.'

What was most difficult for political leaders to accept was the existence of a reproportioned world in which the West no longer predominated and, accordingly, in which any devolution of political authority would not be the result of French grant or concession, but the outcome of local force or right. The monarchical approach to republican affairs was always evident in colonial matters, and so it remained until the end. In a speech he made on 11 April 1961, Charles de Gaulle described the first person singularity of it all: 'I granted independence to the mandated states of Syria and Lebanon,' he declared. 'I, along with my Government . . . recognized and aided the independence of the young States in Black Africa . . .,' he continued. 'I proclaimed the right of the Algerian populations to self-determination,' he went on.[3]

The lofty tone of this rhetoric did not mean that de Gaulle was not a close observer of the local scene, that he did not respond effectively when necessary. Certainly he did, his role in ending the Algerian war for independence and in the transfer of power to the former African colonies being a most significant one. But what his language suggests, what the legislation of the time demonstrates was the cultural and historical inequality that most French assumed existed in world affairs.

France was seen as more than a nation, something more imposing than a political entity; it was a cultural force. In imperialist rhetoric, France had a 'vocation'. This quasi-religious term was the defending noun of empire. Even as late as 1959, when he recognised that empire was no longer feasible anywhere, Charles de Gaulle, visiting Dakar, Senegal, in his capacity of president of the new Fifth Republic, qualified his nation's political attitude in the time-honoured way: 'From its very inception, the vocation of France, the purpose of France have been a humane vocation and a humane purpose,' he declared.[4]

When joined by other mystical words like 'faith', 'trust', and 'belief', the vocabulary of imperialism became ethereal and mist-like, floating above political corridor and marketplace. Aside from the often repeated statistic of '100,000,000 Frenchmen', used to give the empire well-rounded significance, the French policymakers seldom dealt in numbers. Theirs was no collection of territories explained by a 'balance sheet of empire'; it was, they assumed, a grouping of peoples joined by strong, if invisible bonds of devotion.

Many examples of this imagined relationship are easily found, but two are particularly timely because they appeared in print in the year of victory, 1945. Robert Delavignette, then the most respected colonial administrator in France, asserted in the introduction to a book celebrating the men who had founded the French empire, that the wartime experience had bonded French and indigenous soldiers together in sentiment by generating 'a faith that suggested the indivisibility of France Overseas'.[5] The Cambodian political leader, Prince Sisowath Youtevong, contributing to a work entitled *La Communauté impériale française*, published in 1945, insisted that no one should find in the imperial relationship 'a sort of fatalism or resignation on the part of the conquered'. Rather the analyst should understand that what has resulted from this 'life in common, fully accepted or not, are not the shackles of servitude but the links of love. Thus the condition goes beyond the material to the transcendent . . . .'[6]

It should not be surprising to find, after reading such meta-physical assertions, that even the Preamble to the Constitution of the Fourth Republic had sentimental touches. In part the preamble reads: 'Faithful to its traditional mission, France intends to lead the peoples in its charge to the freedom by which they can administer themselves and democratically run their own affairs . . . .'

The phrase 'intends to lead' was, of course, soon at variance with the facts. The singular characteristic of the Fourth Republic's history in colonial affairs was the lack of sustained and well-directed leadership.

POLITICS, CONSTITUTION-MAKING, AND COLONIAL RELATIONSHIPS IN THE FORMATION OF THE FOURTH REPUBLIC

The first two decades of the postwar era, which were also the terminal ones of colonial empire, were marked in France by efforts at domestic reconstruction and efforts to prevent colonial disintegration. As the French nation tried to recover from the war and to modernise, it also responded fitfully to the political clamour and militant behaviour from abroad by colonial reform and then by acceptance of independence.

Described as a hexagon, a term that suggests fixity and order, France was a nation in flux, at home, on the Continent and in the world. Postwar readjustment began with the cleaning up of the shattering experience of World War II. There was, first, the severe domestic discomfort of a war-dislocated economy, of fuel and housing shortages, of the need for new capital formation and of reconstruction of a delapidated infrastructure, above all the railroad system. There was also the new chill of the Cold War, in which the domestic French Communist Party dutifully followed the ideological lead of Moscow and behaved in a manner seen as disloyal to and subversive of the new republican regime.

Were this not enough, the old political tendencies of party fragmentation and parliamentary compromise returned to plague the Fourth Republic. 'Parliament was supreme but immobile,' wrote one keen observer in a trenchant analysis of the situation.[7] In the game of corridor politics, much energy was expended in forming short-lived governments incapable of initiating and implementing major reform.

Almost as if subscribing to Caesar's famous remark that Gaul was divided into three parts, the French parliamentary arrangement under the Fourth Republic was tripartite. Indeed, the term 'Third

Force' (duly capitalised) was popular immediately after the war, a term employed to describe a centrist effort to provide balance between the Right and the Left. Yet most of the political parties were only recently formed, amalgamations from the war experience. The chief exceptions were the Socialists and the Communists, but the bothersome element was the French Communist Party which, essentially assuming the posture and ideology of Moscow, was considered a domestic threat and, beginning in 1947, was effectively excluded from governmental power. While the Communists occupied the far Left position, the Gaullists, first joined in the Rally of the French People (RPF), were on the Right. In the middle, and in a rather fluid state, were the old Socialist Party and the newly-emerged Popular Republican Movement (MRP), a variant of the Christian Socialist Parties in other countries. Without exceptional leadership, and without the collective parliamentary experience of the pre-war political parties, most of these parties had to suffer compromise, just as they had to strive for coalition, in order to exercise some semblance of political authority. The term which was then devised to explain and criticise this condition was *immobilisme*, a condition of national political paralysis.

At the very time that they were organising their parties, the new leaders were confronted with the need for a new constitution because the Third Republic and its institutions had been cast aside along with other debris of the war. During this crucial year of debate and resolution, 1946, the Communist Party played an important role in the activities of the Constituent Assembly, intensifying political instability and, it should be added, intensifying the often strident tone of the discussions that were concerned with the establishment of the constitution of the Fourth Republic.

What was at issue in colonial matters was chiefly the federal principle. Initially discussed in 1942 in the Consultative Assembly of de Gaulle's provisional government sitting in Algiers, and then again during the Brazzaville Conference of 1944, when a federal assembly was suggested, federation was a new institutional departure for the French. The newness was not only of overarching principle but, obviously, of integrating administration. During the long term of the Third Republic, colonial administration had developed unconnectedly through individual treaties, through the imaginative rule of a few able administrators and between the Ministry of Colonies and the Ministry of Foreign Affairs. Like the

British Empire, the French was not unified under a single agency or through a clearly articulated hierarchy of command. Only one principle prevailed: domination by France.

Now this principle was changed, at least on paper. The Preamble to the Constitution of the Fourth Republic read: 'France forms with the overseas peoples, a union founded on the equality of rights and responsibilities, without distinction of race or religion'. The old empire, which had been unitary in myth and diverse in fact, was now replaced by a Union that was federal in myth and confused in practice. The confusion resulted from the French discomfort with the implications of the term 'equality of rights and responsibilities'. If literally interpreted, then France would no longer stand apart from and above the overseas territories. As the old republican figure and longtime mayor of Lyons, Edouard Herriot, decried when the granting of citizenship to all the indigenous peoples was proposed during the constitutional debates: 'France would become the colony of its former colonies' under such an arrangement.[8]

In the draft constitution provided by the First Constituent Assembly, the so-called April (1946) draft, all the overseas territories and member states 'form a union based on free consent'. This new French Union would be comprised of three broad groupings: the old colonies (Guadeloupe and Martinique in the Caribbean, Réunion in the Indian Ocean, St Pierre and Miquelon in the Atlantic) and Algeria which already formed French departments, the 'Associated States' (those with which France had treaty arrangements: Tunisia, Morocco and Indochina), and the overseas territories (the former 'colonies', notably in West Africa).

In principle the new structure by which the various units were assembled was matched by a series of political reforms. Article 44 in effect removed colonial status for all the people in the old empire and conferred on them 'the rights of citizenship'. Local legislative assemblies were to be instituted, with membership elected directly and on the principle of universal suffrage. Although there was to be a Council of the French Union, the debate over such a second legislative body aroused anxiety over its possible conservative role, a matter of concern to the indigenous representatives from the overseas territories and to the Communists. By the time the constitution was completed, the Council was reduced to little more than a consultative body.

In many ways a radical departure from the principles of the old colonial empire, the Union was federal only by the qualifying adjective. The old assimilationist tendency continued, even if a degree of local political autonomy was to be granted. The old revolutionary principle of central authority and universality was reasserted; the constitution stated that the republic 'is one and indivisible'.

While the overseas representatives urged their constituents to vote for the constitution and the vast majority did so, the French metropolitan electorate rejected the Constitution in a referendum held on 5 May 1946 and, therefore, a Second Constitutent Assembly was formed.

The second constitution seemed to be more federal in structure. The French Union now had a Federal Assembly seated in Paris, to which representatives from the overseas territories, as well as the departments, were elected. A High Council of the French Union, comprised of representatives of the Associated States and of the French government was also created. And the president of the Republic also became the president of the French Union.

The new Constitution papered over growing differences emerging from deep disappointments. The political system and the processes by which it operated were to be flexible, evolutionary in the opinion of the indigenous representatives from the overseas territories. Article 75 of the revised and accepted constitution did declare that the status of members of the French Union 'is capable of evolution', an article included to satisfy – or pacify – these representatives. However, the local assemblies were denied any real power and the new Federal Assembly was but a consultative body. The French National Assembly, in the earlier parliamentary tradition, was responsible for legislation that concerned the overseas territories.

What the French Union was not was a federation. For some of the African representatives the Union should have been a confederation, thereby allowing political development and change over a twenty-year period, which individuals like Léopold Sédar Senghor considered the length of time required to determine the final nature of the new structure. To most of the French politicians, the Union was a liberal, redesignated colonial system from which archaic terms were removed and some semblance of equality was allowed, but in which the French government still was to exercise sovereignty. Put in traditional physical terms, the centripetal power of France was maintained. What the French Union lacked was the one element that could have assured its success: the free consent of the indigenous populations.[9]

THE COLONIAL REACTION TO CONSTITUTIONAL REFORM

What those populations then anticipated in new or reformed political structure was not at all clear. Few of the territories yet had anything approaching popular political movements, let alone well-articulated expressions of national protest. The persistent concerns and expressions of discontent had centred on taxes and wages, on imposed services and severe judicial policies, such as the *indigénat*. Certainly, new sentiments and concerns were arising, inspired by the education given to some, urged on by returning servicemen who now better understood the inequities in the colonial system and the forms of discrimination it tolerated. With the establishment of trade unions and with the development of literacy of sufficient proportions to support the publication of politically-oriented newspapers, what the French call *journaux d'opinion*, something of a public temper was developing in the colonial world.

Even under the weight of these new conditions, there was no structure-threatening strain observable to the French. On the contrary, they took comfort in the commentary of many of the indigenous representatives elected to the Constituent Assembly and serving on the committee charged with colonial reform. Many of these persons spoke of unity and cooperation, not of revolution and independence. Senghor, future president of the Republic of Senegal and at this earlier time special *rapporteur* of the proposed articles relating to the French Union, spoke of a 'marriage, not an association' of the various territories. Fili-Dabo Sissoko, a representative from the Sudan exclaimed, 'I am proud to be French'. Even the Algerian leader Ferhat Abbas, said, 'No one is asking France to leave. We need the nation'.[10]

Just as the French themselves were politically divided, so the leadership of the overseas territories had no clear unity of purpose, no common objective of liberation. Indochina was off by itself in political geography and political behaviour, as the revolutionary elements there began their struggle against French domination. Ferhat Abbas had already asked that Algeria be a sovereign nation, and a representative from Madagascar had tried, by the introduction of a bill that was not considered, to turn that colony into 'a free state' within the French Union. Senghor and the African representatives wanted a flexible, a 'dynamic' system, which would allow evolutionary change.

The intense and varied interest in the French Union expressed by the overseas representatives was not matched by the French, for whom the status of the French Union was neither a pressing nor a primary consideration. Yet the constitutional developments were somewhat altered between the two constituent assemblies when political power gravitated more to the Centre in France and when political opposition coalesced among the indigenous representatives. Now the newly formed MRP was the dominant element in the French government with Georges Bidault as its premier. Bidault intruded into the Constituent Assembly's deliberations and offered proposals that were viewed by many as retrogressive, among which special representation for French colonists and a revision of the proposed common citizenship were prominent.

This latter issue was one of keen concern because it was the basic condition of the assimilationist approach. In the first constitutional draft, Article 44 stated that 'French dependents of the metropolis and overseas territories enjoy the rights of citizenship' as do the French at home. When that draft was rejected in the referendum, one of the Senegalese representatives, Lamine-Guèye, had what was called the 'Lamine Guèye Law' passed on 7 May 1946, a law which guaranteed French citizenship to these peoples. Bidault's terminology was of less than that crystal-clear quality which practitioners of the French language admire. In his plan, the new Assembly of the Union would have special representation for 'persons holding French civil status', a phrase that greatly displeased the French school teacher who was Léopold Senghor.

This dual retreat from liberal reform – the indirect reintroduction of the principle of a dual college system of election and the weakening of the status of common citizenship – was fought by the newly formed Intergroup of Indigenous Deputies. Thirty-eight of the 63 overseas representatives, these persons bonded together in reaction to the rejection of the April Draft of the Constitution, the one that had pleased them.

Bringing pressure on the MRP government, the Intergroup forced a change in Bidault's position and the removal of the two particular clauses that irritated. However, when Bidault praised the revised political and electoral arrangements that the Second Constituent Assembly had incorporated into the structure of the French Union by declaring that 'we have established a foundation unlike any other in the world . . . a great community, a single community, under a common flag',[11] the members of the Intergroup of Indigenous Representatives, sitting together, collectively restrained from applause.

THE FRENCH EMPIRE IN A NEW INTERNATIONAL LIGHT

There were likewise no loud sounds of applause from abroad for this statement, nor were there many expressions of accordance with whatever the French were doing in their territories in those early postwar years. Although complaints and protests are easily found among the literature of colonialism in the interwar period, a pronounced or concerted effort against the activity never was made. The war experience changed that. One instance, recounted as an anecdote occurring during the Teheran Conference of 1943, was demonstrable proof of the new tendency. When Prime Minister Winston Churchill protested a statement made by President Franklin D. Roosevelt about the reprehensible behaviour of the French in Indochina and therefore the need to establish a trusteeship over the region, Roosevelt snapped, 'Now, look Winston, you are outvoted three to one'.[12]

If in this instance Roosevelt was referring to the concurring opinion of Joseph Stalin of the Soviet Union and Chiang Kai-shek of the Republic of China, such protest of colonialism by public declaration and by a show of hands was a common characteristic of international conferences and in world press opinion after World War II.

Empire then appeared to be at best an archaic form of rule, an uneconomical and oppressive one at worse. Clearly inconsistent with the principles of self-determination which had first been made part of the international political vocabulary by Woodrow Wilson and which were later reiterated by President Franklin D. Roosevelt in the Atlantic Charter of 1941, self-determination was in the late twentieth century what liberty had been in the late eighteenth, a word of hope, a word of command. Already those qualities were found in the prefatory statement to Ferhat Abbas's 'Manifesto of the Algerian People', which stated that the subsequently listed demands were based on President Roosevelt's assurance that 'in the organization of a new world, the rights of all peoples, large and small, would be respected'. A decade later, in 1955, representatives of half of the world's population, that large portion only recently dominated or manipulated by the West, met at Bandung, Indonesia, in the first Conference of Asian-African Countries and declared:

> The right of self-determination must be enjoyed by all peoples, and freedom and independence must be granted, with the least possible delay to those who are still dependent peoples.

By this time most of Southeast Asia, including Indochina, sat at the conference as independent states, as these same states sat in the General Assembly of the United Nations where they regularly protested colonialism.

During its formation in 1944 and 1945, this new world organisation, which had replaced the League of Nations and later would develop into an agency of considerable influence, took up the issue of trusteeship, a new term expressing a different set of conditions of responsibility for what had earlier been the mandate system. The American government had proposed the general idea in a position paper from the Secretary of State, Cordell Hull, to President Franklin D. Roosevelt, which was dated 9 March 1943, and in which Hull recommended that the United Nations be 'charged with responsibilities for the future of colonial areas', a charge which meant helping them become 'qualified for independent national status'.[13]

Initially opposed and then, later, reluctantly accepted by the British government, the idea was disturbing to the French. Their response to the American 'Working Paper' on the subject, circulated for consideration in the spring of 1944, was most critical because of the condition of self-government it recommended. The French preferred the more unconstraining notion of 'progressive development of political institutions'. Although the accepted version of the principle of trusteeship did not require any colonial power to place its current possessions under such supervision – this requirement was restricted only to territories formerly held by the enemy and to the older mandated territories – French opposition demonstrated the reluctance of the government to accept liberalising change.

In this and in other colonial matters, the United Nations did not so much disturb French colonial affairs as inconvenience the national government. Far more significant was the effect on 'the other side'. The deliberations of the General Assembly gave heart and voice to the colonial movements for liberation.

At the end of the first decade of the postwar era and some time around the meeting of the Bandung Conference, the idea of a 'Third World' – peoples and nations of different status and aspirations from the 'first world' of the United States and capitalism and the 'second world' of the Soviet Union and Stalinist communism – was proposed. The idea often implied non-alignment with either of the superpower 'blocs', but it always implied a commonality of experience, of a shared history of those people forcefully made 'the wretched of the earth'. The phrase is the title of one of the most influential criticisms of colonialism, whose author was Frantz Fanon, born in Martinique, educated in France and who served as a medical doctor in the FLN (National Liberation Front) in the early years of the Algerian war.

Fanon created a global historical process which he had extrapolated from what he had seen and experienced in Algeria and which he had had enriched with the results of his own reading in existentialism and modern psychology. The 'Third World finds itself and speaks to itself through his voice', wrote the famous French existentialist thinker Jean-Paul Sartre in the preface to the book.[14] Fanon's global assessment of the colonial experience was made without ambiguity, with none of the nuances that were now so familiar in French writings concerned with the subject. 'The colonial world is a Manichean world,' Fanon argued, in which 'the settler paints the native as a sort of quintessence of evil'.[15] Fanon's historically-set conclusion was severe: colonialism had occurred through an act of violence and could only be ended by an act of violence. Not negotiation but action was required, a sort of purification by fire which would eradicate old colonial institutions and the compromising attitudes that they engendered so as to make possible the national regeneration of the colonised peoples.

Charged with emotion and expressed with bitterness, Fanon's powerful book called for liberation. Self-generated force from the oppressed people, not concession from or compromise with the decaying colonial administration, was the only means by which to acquire national dignity and national entity, Fanon insisted.

Originally written in French, first published by a radical French editor, *The Wretched of the Earth*, supposedly written for Third World peoples, was imperatively commended to a European audience by Sartre: 'Europeans, you must open this book and enter into it'.[16]

Few did, even though by the date of its publication, 1961, the colonial enterprise was all but over. Before then, there had been colonial struggle, some of it not dissimilar to what Fanon found necessary, but there also had been much negotiation and compromise. If there is one generalisation that sweeps across empire, it is this: the Europeans retreated from empire. Certainly, they were forced back by arms, but they also stepped back through negotiation. None of the acts of political devolution in the colonial worlds was done very gracefully because the one quality unforeseen by either side was the rapidity of the change. What has been called 'the terminal decade' of imperialism was a span of time somewhat longer for the French than for the British. The war in Indochina began in 1946 and the negotiations over the independence of Algeria concluded in 1962.

Viewed retrospectively and globally, the end of colonial empire seemed to be a process, hence the term 'decolonization'. Unique as an experience to the individual peoples involved, and varying according to the nature of the institutions and responses employed, decolonisation was described as the falling apart or the breaking up of empire, parts of a whole changing position and status.

The particular acts and actions, the efforts to prevent the consequences of one situation from affecting another, the argument of uniqueness for what occurred in a place like Algeria – all can be subsumed under the overarching phenomenon. As if responding to the physical law of inertia, decolonisation, once begun, continued, was incapable of being arrested. In the sequence which marked the end of most of *France d'Outre-Mer*, the form geographically resembled a scimitar. From Indochina, the movement swept westward to North Africa, then around to West Africa and on down to Equatorial Africa.

Given its grand scale, its far-reaching implications and its long-enduring effects, the history of the collapse of modern French colonial empire begs the search for an appropriate epigram. Such a one might be this: the French seized on empire at the very moment it was slipping from their grasp.

6 Dissolution

In the drama of French colonialism, the last scene of military celebration occurred on Bastille Day, 1957. Then, the 10th Para Division, under the command of General Jacques Massu, marched smartly along the Champs-Elysées in Paris. The rugged looking soldiers, their red berets fixed at a jaunty angle, the sleeves of their camouflaged tunics rolled up and their submachine guns slung over their shoulders, these soldiers made a fine impression and were greeted with cheers.

Massu and his troops had returned from Algeria where, on 7 January 1957, they had been given the responsibility and unlimited authority for assuring peace in the capital city of Algiers, at the time that its social life was disrupted by militant action and its French residents both indignant and terrified. With brutal efficiency, Massu had executed his charge. And so it appeared, certainly to the French lining the Champs-Elysées on that Bastille Day, that Massu had succeeded in turning the battle for his country. Algeria would remain French.

At this inconsequential moment in French colonial history, the French had put behind them the disastrous military experience in Indochina, an experience still bitterly remembered however by Massu and many of his soldiers who had previously served there. To them and others, Algeria would not be another Indochina: the lessons of that war had been learned and French tactics adjusted to the new conditions of guerrilla fighting. What had not yet been learned was the outdatedness of the colonial posture. No matter how outfitted, the French presence was seen as foreign domination, a condition of previous times already overwhelmed and overturned by World War II.

Reluctant imperialists, the French politicians continued to be reluctant to call it quits, 'to scram out of Africa' in the nice play on words of imperialist history, 'the scramble for Africa', suggested by the Kenyan Tom Mboya.

Now, in North Africa, as before in Southeast Asia, the French response to colonial demands was dual and inconsistent: indecision

78

and action, parliamentary debate and military action. Neither prepared philosophically nor psychologically for the end of empire, neither sufficiently knowledgeable about local conditions nor politically strong enough to pursue a well-directed, forceful policy, the French leadership moved to an uncertain future, somewhat hopeful of one development: the finding of a temporary solution by which empire, under whatever guise and of whatever territory, might continue.

All proposed solutions were poorly timed. Never before in the records of history had the future tense so suddenly become the present tense. Not only the French but all of the colonial powers, as well as most of the indigenous leaders opposed to colonialism, were amazed at the rapidity with which colonial authority was dissolved. In 1946, for instance, Léopold Sédar Senghor spoke of a dynamic time of 20 years in which the constitutional arrangements for the colonial empire would evolve. Twenty years later, he had already completed four years as president of the Republic of Senegal.

A few years, not several decades, marked the march of events, timing that further aggravated the indecisiveness of the politicians and confounded the intentions of the militarists who attempted to command France's destiny. It all began, this confusing process so simply described by the term 'decolonization', in Indochina. Previous to the outbreak of colonial war there, all anti-colonial acts had been manageable, however awkward and inconvenient they had appeared. Although General de Gaulle in 1943 declared the French intention to return as sovereign to Indochina, the French never regained a sure footing there. Their political acts were ineffectual, and their military efforts were futile.

EFFORTS AT NEGOTIATION AND COMPROMISE IN INDOCHINA

The final years of the French presence in that South Asian peninsula were marked by war, at once colonial in operation and international in implication.[1] That the French could attempt to reassert themselves as the dominant power in what they had politically labelled 'Indochina' was in large part the result of the changed American attitude toward French colonialism. President Roosevelt, just before his death, had relented on his severe anticolonialism in deference to

Churchill and that prime minister's concern for the British empire. Then, with the presidency of Harry S. Truman, a more favourable American attitude emerged, both because Truman had no interest in colonial affairs and because the spectre of Communism was soon seen by the Americans to hover over Southeast Asia. Advisers to the American president developed the 'domino theory' of possible results, the fear that the fall of one Southeastern Asia state to Communism would lead to the same fate for another, the action possibly reaching around the world to Europe. The French, soon capitalising on this feared exercise in political mechanics, sought financial aid from the Americans to carry out a war more costly than the Fourth Republic could comfortably bear.

Although initially reluctant to assume any involvement in this Indochinese imbroglio but also anxious to have the French continue to resist Communism, the Americans did eventually provide financial, as well as logistical support, and thus began, however indirectly, American involvement that would lead to another Vietnam War, after the French had left in defeat.[2]

Further distinguishing this war was the fact that it was fought by two armies using different methods and proclaiming different principles. For the Vietminh, the nationalist and Communist – for they were both – forces galvanised by Ho Chi Minh and directed by Vo Nugyen Giap, the history teacher who became a brilliant practitioner of guerrilla warfare, the war was directed to national unification by liberation from foreign domination. For the French the war was a reassertion of their paramountcy and was, in effect, a nineteenth-century colonial war in disposition, fought by an expeditionary corps, officered by the French but largely soldiered by North Africans, Vietnamese and the Foreign Legion.

The spirit, intention and effect of the French military enterprise were later summarised, after the final defeat, by a French journalist, Lucien Bodard, who related in his *The Quicksand War: Prelude to Vietnam* (1967), part of a conversation he had had in Hong Kong with two American journalists. Analysing the defeat, one said: 'But I admire your army. They know how to make a *beau geste*'. The statement caused Bodard to reflect:

> It was kind of him, no doubt, but he really meant that the French army, like a Louis Quinze armchair, was the masterpiece of an extinct civilization.[3]

The chief, the fatal French anachronism was what might be called the colonial attitude: the assumption that the indigenous population could be controlled, if not won over. Some war and some reform were the imperatives – if the meaning of that word may be diluted – of French policy in Indochina. Neither one nor the other of these two activities was ever strong enough to be effective. The French neither 'mopped up' nor 'muddled through'.

From the time they returned to the time they finally left, the French were on unsettled territory. Local dissatisfaction and international competition were the consistent conditions which further aggravated the French effort to reassert domination. These conditions predated the triumphal entry of General Leclerc into Saigon in October 1945, where he stood as France's intention to set things aright.

Indochina had been in, but was not actually part of the Pacific War. Its administration, loyal to the Vichy Regime, had been rather effectively manoeuvred into a position of isolation by Governor-General Decoux. What he had done was to make the best of a bad situation during the war. In acceding to Japanese requests to station troops in Indochina and to use the communications systems there for the movement of supplies to the war fronts, Decoux had managed to retain a semblance of sovereignty and to maintain a high degree of order: the Vietnamese had remain acquiescent. Then, suddenly and brutally, the Japanese occupied the country on 9 March 1945, removed and imprisoned the French and encouraged the Annamite emperor Bao Dai to establish a national government independent of French rule. Bao Dai, who had been emperor since 1925, saw this as the occasion to assert Vietnamese control over local affairs – as he also saw no alternative to the Japanese demand disguised as a request. The Japanese granted one major concession: the incorporation of Cochinchina, the southernmost portion of French Indochina into this new state. Thus, Vietnam was united in principle, its three major units, Annam, Tonkin and Cochinchina under common authority.

What Bao Dai received on paper, Ho Chi Minh was amassing on site. As Japanese authority waned in the last months of the war, and before the Allied Forces made an appearance in Indochina, Ho made this moment of twilight rule his new tomorrow. He successfully gained political control of the country for his Viet Nam Doc Lap Dong Minh Hoi, or League for the Independence of

Vietnam, which was known in abbreviation as Viet Minh. Ho was one of the most elusive, ambitious and ubiquitous of the revolutionary leaders of the time.[4]

Ho's revolutionary career had always been one of touch-and-go, and so it continued through the war. Setting out on a mission to win Chinese support, he was imprisoned and moved about between 1942 and 1943. However, the Chinese reversed their position and eventually gave Ho support. He returned to Indochina in 1944 and prepared for the guerrilla warfare in which he and his cohorts would be most successful. As he declared in establishing the 'Propaganda Unit for National Liberation', the first of his combat units charged with both military and political activity, '... we will apply guerrilla warfare, which consists in being secret, rapid, active, now in the east, now in the west, arriving unexpectedly and leaving unnoticed'.

Ho, hitherto Nguyen Ai Quoc ('Nguyen' being a common Vietnamese patronymic and 'Ai Quoc' generally translated as 'the patriot') took his new name for political reasons and henceforth was styled Ho Chi Minh, 'he who enlightens'. The passive voice would have been better: Ho was enlightened by the situation and began to organise the northern region of Co Bang politically as he asserted his military control over it, this particular task given to Vo Nugyen Giap, who would later lead the Vietminh troops to military victory over the French at Dien Bien Phu.

As the Japanese war effort collapsed, Ho moved to advantage, gaining widespread support from Hanoi to Saigon. On August 23, Bao Dai recognised the isolation of his own regime and, desiring both to assure national unity and a place for himself in the new political order, abdicated. On August 29, Ho declared the 'Provisional Government of the Democratic Republic of Vietnam'.

This was not all the French debarked to find. By Allied agreement, the country had been divided at the 16th parallel, with the Chinese responsible for maintaining order and disarming the Japanese in the north, while the British did the same in the south. Between the two, a small group of Americans, from the Office of Strategic Services, busily roamed. The Saigon to which Leclerc was directed was the centre of the ensuing confusion, yet the one place on the peninsula in which the French were to reassume authority quickly.

Prior to the militant action on 22 September 1945, by which the French regained control, the city was politically confounded: the

British in occupation, the Vietminh in command, the French population in terror. The Committee of the South, the group representing the Vietminh, had taken over the government of the city and had harrassed the French. Now, with the arrival of the British, the French population expected and wanted the situation reversed.

At first hesitant because his orders called for no such intervention, the British commander allowed the small contingent of French troops sent by de Gaulle to release 1000 French soldiers who had been confined to their barracks since the Japanese surrender. This group, now armed with American equipment, ejected the Vietminh government in the city and forced order on the Vietnamese population. Outwardly, Saigon was again the 'Paris of the Far East', and from this elegant base Leclerc, who had arrived on October 5, began his military effort to wipe out the Vietminh, a task he first thought possible in the light of his initial victories. However, he soon realised what every military commander eventually came to know: the French did not have the men or the equipment to achieve decisive victory. The French future in Indochina would have to be negotiated, but from a position of military advantage, it was hoped.

Such a conclusion about his current condition was also reached by Ho, but only as a temporary expedient. Also without sufficient men and equipment to gain military ascendency, disappointed with the lack of American military assistance upon which he had counted, confronted with famine conditions in the territory he controlled and concerned with the presence of the Chinese as military occupiers of the north, Ho entered into negotiations. He signed an accord on 6 March 1946 which established the 'Republic of Vietnam as a Free State, having its own government' within an already established Indochinese Federation.

The act seemed consistent with previously presented, if not established, principles. On 26 March 1945, even before the French had returned to Indochina, the provisional government issued a declaration that established the French Union, this even before the Constitutional Assembly had officially approved it. The Union was to consist of the four states of French Indochina – Vietnam, Cochinchina, Laos and Cambodia. Arranged in a federation which would have a French official – now called High Commissioner – as its chief, and with foreign and military affairs under direct French authority, each state would enjoy a degree of autonomy in its economic matters, and would have its own popularly elected assembly which would be responsible for local affairs. Avoiding any mention of sovereignty and independence, the new French Union was an effort at temporisation: the satisfaction of some indigenous demands for control of their own affairs along with the retention of more than a semblance of French authority.

Into this ill-fitting administrative framework, Ho's 'Republic of Vietnam' was to be placed, but only temporarily. When Ho journeyed to Paris to enter into further discussions with the French government about the status of his recently recognised republic, and while he was being greeted with the ceremony attending a visit of a head of state, his political position in Indochina suffered severe alteration. The claim he had laid to all of Vietnam was, as it were, rescinded. The decision altering the local politics was locally made, without consultation with the national government in Paris. The architect, if that familiar diplomatic metaphor may be used for the person who engineered the ill-structured arrangement, was Admiral Thierry d'Argenlieu, de Gaulle's chief representative as High Commissioner to Indochina.

Personally one of the most unusual political figures in modern times and politically one of the most intransigent, d'Argenlieu had been a monk between the two world wars and then had served with the Free French as a military officer. His politics were as cloistered as he had been. Yet when de Gaulle appointed him to this important and sensitive position, few knew just how intransigent and impetuous he might be.

In a matter of a few months, the Admiral had compromised the French government. As negotiations with Ho Chi Minh were proceeding, d'Argenlieu acted on his own. Disturbed but not dissuaded by Ho's insistence that further negotiations take place in Paris, d'Argenlieu still insisted on a local conference, now imperative, he told the Vietminh, because of the growing desire for autonomy in Cochinchina. Without the presence of Ho or any of his representatives, and following the suggestion of the Advisory Council, which had replaced the Committee of the South, d'Argenlieu unilaterally recognised the Republic of Cochinchina which was granted the same conditions of existence as Ho Chi Minh's provisional government. Thus, even before Ho left for France on May 31, a new regime existed which the government in Paris had little choice but to approve.

Clearly on paper and vaguely in fact, the area of Vietnam now had two separate and competing regimes. Ho bitterly tolerated the situation, returning from France with the promise of further negotiations in 1947 but was soon further angered by the approved constitution of the Fourth Republic which allowed of no free states within the French Union.

MILITARY CONFRONTATION

Tension was acute; peace was fragile. Then, in late 1946, a series of incidents in which both the French and the Vietnamese lost lives in Haiphong, where Ho had concentrated his power, led to open conflagration. What might be called skirmishes were elongated into concentrated military confrontation. Although both sides were responsible for the multiplication of incidents, it was the French action on 23 November 1946 that may be considered the 'outbreak' of the war.

On that day, the French authorities decided to take a firm stand in response to two incidents in which 29 French soldiers had just been killed. An ultimatum was given to the Vietminh to evacuate the quarter of Haiphong in which they were situated. Refusal was met with the deployment of French troops, subsequent gunfire and then the flight of panicked civilians toward the airport, a move hastily misinterpreted by the French as an attack. The French responded by a naval bombardment which resulted in the death of some 6000 civilians.

Even after this action, the French attempted negotiation, while the Vietminh now planned a coordinated attack to dislocate the French in Haiphong. On December 11, the central electricity generating plant was blown up, and, in the darkness, the Vietminh moved against the French population in the city. The engagement began a colonial war, one of the several that marked this decade in Southeast Asian history, but the one that was the longest and perhaps the most brutal.

Broadly speaking, two wars were to develop in the peninsula: the first was the French which took place in what was then called Indochina; the second was the American in what had become Vietnam. The transition between the two was made ideologically when the colonial justification was replaced by an anti-

Communist one. That transition occurred in 1949, more specifically on March 9, when the French government granted full independence to the 'Republic of Vietnam', again headed by the ever-accessible Bao Dai. What Bao received in political authority was exactly what Ho Chi Minh had demanded and been denied: sovereignty. Henceforth, the French justified their military presence in Cold War terms, as a nation seeking to stem the red tide in Southeast Asia by supporting a sovereign state fighting Communism.

The French could mark their reasoning on the local map. In 1949, the Communist government of Mao Tse-tung had finally defeated the forces of Chiang Kai-shek. Communist troops moved quickly to the northern border of Vietnam. In another year, when North Korea invaded South Korea in June, 1950, the 'Cold War' was extended as a hot one to Asia.

The French now were ideologically joined with the Americans as defenders of the 'Free World', perceived as pitted against a relentless, ever-encroaching, Soviet-directed Communism. In a remarkable article published in October 1950, about five months after the outbreak of the Korean War, Jacques Soustelle, a long-standing Gaullist and a strong colonialist, stated what he considered to be the proper perspective on the international scene:

> The conflict in Indo-China thus is not between France and the Viet-Minh. That is only a local manifestation of the resistance of peoples on the periphery of Asia to the Soviet expansion from the heart of the continent, directed toward the peninsulas of the Pacific.[5]

Soustelle's perception had already become that of the Americans. Gone was any further reference to rapacious French colonialism. Now, new words of approval were supported by needed military assistance. Both the Truman and the Eisenhower administrations responded to the French, not just because of the accepted domino theory but also because of political complications in Europe, where the Americans desired approval by the French National Assembly of a European Defence Community, a joint military force to stand ready to prevent a Soviet takeover, a fear of considerable proportions at the time. American support in Indochina, it was hoped, would engender support for the military force proposed for Europe.

The French therefore fought in Indochina with ever-increasing and always desired American military aid and with ever-increasing but never desired American military advice. It was an uncomfortable arrangement, and it yielded no effective results.

Although it appeared initially that the French had the military advantage because of their organisation and modern equipment, notably tanks and aircraft, it was soon seen that they lacked popular support, knowledge of the terrain and appreciation of the tenacity of the Vietminh forces. Therefore, the initial military intention to drive the Vietminh northward from their major bases in Tonkin was frustrated, notably along the line of principal action, Colonial Route 4, which linked Langson to Caobang, on the northernmost border of Indochina with China.

Following a proposed strategy of developing 'hedgehogs', well-armed outposts that were considered military self-sufficient and capable of disrupting enemy activities, the French so armed Caobang and thereupon deemed it impregnable. What had not yet been evaluated was the general change in Vietminh tactics.

General Giap was a theorist as well as a practitioner, a student who had examined Napoleon's strategy and who knew the nature of modern warfare. He envisaged a three-part development in what was called a war of national liberation: spontaneous guerrilla warfare, organised guerrilla warfare and, then, a modern war of movement with well-organised and equipped units. 1950 was the year that the third stage had been reached.

By that time the new Chinese Communist regime was supplying Giap with weapons and equipment by means of convoys moving over hastily constructed roads that connected China with Vietminh-held territory. Trucks, artillery and machine guns were abundant enough for the Vietminh to equip three major divisions, the ones that would carry the war effectively against the French. Although the French command was aware of these developments, the sudden use of new tactics of mass warfare, carried out with adequate fire power, was unexpected. The old colonial mentality was difficult to alter.

Yet the confidence which arose from that mentality quickly evaporated in the first week of October, 1950. Then, the French positions along Colonial Route 4 were attacked and destroyed. Caobang had to be evacuated, but only after the French Legionnaires had attempted to destroy all that might be useful to the enemy in the city.

The high command's exercise in military addition was bleak: the miserable retreat from Caobang, plus the Vietminh military success against other French outposts amounted to the total failure of the command of the French Expeditionary Force to succeed against this first full Vietminh attack. 1950 was the year in which the French were denied any opportunity for victory.

Only one extended moment of military enthusiasm and hope of success occurred in the following year, when General Jean de Lattre de Tassigny took command of the expeditionary forces and assumed the title of High Commissioner as well. One of France's finest generals, a powerful, if enigmatic personality, de Lattre moved briskly and apparently successfully. He forced the establishment of a Vietnamese army, envisaged in the accords that had established the republic now headed by Bao Dai. Moreover, de Lattre travelled to Washington where he managed to convince the political leadership that France was in Indochina for global, not for particular French reasons, that the war was one against Communism. His words were translated into more military support for France.

Militarily, de Lattre used his now well-equipped army to fight the Vietminh on the northern plains. His new and bold action badly harrassed Giap's forces, causing large losses of men and forcing Vietminh retreat from territory that they held northwest of Hanoi. De Lattre went further, both building a ring of concrete forts along the northern border and then shifting from the defensive posture that the French had previously assumed to an offensive one, this to win over both French and American opinion, increasingly doubtful of the quality of the military effort.

In his last measured move, de Lattre set out to occupy Hao Binh, a town that he intended to make serve as an outpost from which to interrupt Vietminh supply lines. The attack was successful; the French had penetrated deep into enemy territory. De Lattre then returned to France, already a man suffering from fatal illness. Shortly after his death, the Vietminh, at a great loss of life, forced the French to retreat from Hao Binh. The experience, the history of that military operation, would take on special significance in another two years. Then it would appear, as did Caobang, as a preliminary act to the dreadful defeat the French suffered at Dien Bien Phu.

DIEN BIEN PHU

The end of the French colonial presence in Indochina came in a whirl of confusing negotiation, hastily contrived military planning and disastrous defeat in the years 1953–54.[6] It all was conditioned by an increasing opinion in France that the only solution to the war was negotiation.

On the war front, however, the high command proceeded as best it could. The Expeditionary Force was now composed chiefly of Vietnamese troops and, through negotiations with the Eisenhower administration in Washington in the summer of 1953, some 70% of the financial burden of the war was assumed by the Americans. This internationalisation of the military effort did little to change strategy, again of a defensive nature.

The last French military commander, who assumed his duties in 1953, was General Henri Navarre, trained as a cavalry officer but not previously holding a field command. Navarre wished to regroup, rebuild and increase the numbers of the forces under his command. He also hoped to transfer more of the defensive activities to the Vietnamese troops so that the Expeditionary Force would be able to concentrate on more mobile, offensive action. However, Navarre wanted no major confrontations during the year he anticipated necessary to achieve these results. Yet he took one bold and incautious action: the reoccupation and reinforcement of Dien Bien Phu, in the northwest corner of Tonkin. Viewed strategically as a means of interrupting Vietminh military activity then extending into Laos, and, perhaps, as a means of drawing the Vietminh into an attack that could be effectively defeated, this outpost, another 'hedgehog', seemed capable of being easily supplied from the air and thus effectively maintained. Made-up of five separate outposts rimming the central position where two airstrips were located, the place was manned by 12 000 of the best troops the French had at their disposal.

Shortly after the French had undertaken the military reoccupation of the area on 20 November 1954, diplomatic efforts at resolving the South Asian problem were mounted far off in Berlin. There, a meeting of the four major powers – the United States, the Soviet Union, Great Britain and France – had been called to resolve the issue of European rearmament, of which the European Defence

Community was still the most discussed element. While the conference achieved little on that matter, the Soviet suggestion of another conference in Geneva in May to consider the Far East was warmly greeted by the French, if coldly viewed by the United States, particularly as the Soviets wanted to include Mao's China.

The French had now concluded that the Indochinese War had to be negotiated to an end. This assessment was reinforced by the acceptable conditions of the truce reached between the contending forces in Korea at Panmunjom on 27 June 1953, an agreement which led to the recognised division of that country into two separate states.

Ho Chi Minh was disconcerted by the news of the conference for he feared negotiation would allow the French a more favourable position than they could achieve on the battlefield. By this time, however, both military forces were exhausted so that Ho had no false illusions about 'throwing the French into the sea'.

What the forthcoming Geneva Conference created for the combatants in Indochina was a special problem of timing: what to be done until the conference was seated. For the French, this became a period during which they had to hold on militarily with no severe loss of position. For General Giap this was the time in which to achieve a major military victory of such striking proportions that it would assure the Vietminh a very commanding argument at the negotiation table.

The hands of the clock pointed to Dien Bien Phu. The hour of engagement was deafeningly announced on the night of March 13–14, when the Vietminh artillery surrounding Dien Bien Phu opened fire and Vietminh troops launched the first of their attacks. From that unexpected moment – the first time the Vietminh had begun an attack with heavy artillery – until the last French forces capitulated on May 7, the outpost was under siege, unsusceptible to relief because the airstrips had quickly come under Vietminh fire. Only erratic air drops were possible, such that the camp took on the appearance of the classic situation in colonial fiction: the besieged defence post waiting for relief.

As the Vietminh forces delivered their decimating blows to the French troops, General Paul Ely, Chief-of-Staff of the French Army, negotiated in Washington, initially for more equipment, but then, as the French were threatened with annihilation at Dien Bien Phu, for air support. In Hanoi, French and American military commanders had drawn up a plan for strong American air support,

'Operation Vulture', which was to bring 60 World War II B-29 bombers from the Philippines, to be escorted by carrier-based fighters, so as to saturate the Vietminh position with bombs. However, the plan died quickly in discussion because the response in Washington was hesitant and doubtful.[7] The engagement of American prestige, just after the stalemate conclusion in Korea, the sentiment that the French had not tried hard enough to achieve military victory, the consideration that any escalation of the war should be prefaced by greater American military control and the doubt felt by some generals and advisers that 'Operation Vulture' could even achieve its objective – all of these concerns weighed together to crush the project.

Rebuffed by Congressional leaders in an effort to gain support for possible unilateral American military engagement in Indochina, the Eisenhower Administration attempted to gain international commitment and therefore sought British involvement, a condition that Churchill would only consider after the Geneva Conference. This outcome, aggravated by strong differences with the French on the course of action to be followed, caused the American government to do nothing further but lament the situation.

The French capitulated on 7 May 1954. Although the French expeditionary force was then regrouped and new defensive positions assumed, the war was in effect over. Both sides were exhausted, but the one rejoiced in victory as the other despaired in defeat. There remains one particular ironic element now found in the victory letter Ho Chi Minh wrote on May 8 'on the occasion of the glorious victory of Dien Bien Phu'. In that letter he said: 'The victory is a resounding one, but it is only the beginning ... . Whether our struggle is on the military or diplomatic plane, we shall have to fight long and hard before victory is achieved'.[8] Ho, of course, was not anticipating the long war that would occur after the French had left, when the Americans became seriously engaged in 1956 and remained in battle until 1975. But success against the French now came easily after the victory at Dien Bien Phu.

THE END OF INDOCHINA AND THE SUCCESS OF VIETNAM

At the subsequent Geneva Conference, France ended by international negotiation what it had been unable to achieve by institutional change or by military force.[9] Vietnam was temporarily divided at the 17th Parallel, with the Vietminh recognised in the north and the Republic of Vietnam in the south until a general election was held in June 1956 to determine the unified government. Before then, however, the United States began providing military advisers and more military assistance to the republic in the South. In many ways, the American experience would replicate that of the French, a war fought without clear purpose and objective, lacking strong support and persistent interest from home, undertaken by troops whose efforts were unappreciated, and directed by military commanders who underestimated the tenacity and the fervour of the enemy.

What had particularly complicated, indeed confused, the French military effort in Indochina was the political instability of the Fourth Republic and the more obvious European problems, the one ironic one being rearmament. The French Indochinese War was essentially colonial, an effort to reimpose French rule, to reassert France's position as a great, a global power. Yet as the French struggled, they only succeeded in strengthening the anti-colonial movements. The political unrest in Cambodia and Laos had been exploited by the Vietminh which had forces in both countries and which had established a United Front of the three countries in 1950. Although this latter organisation was more sham than substance, its existence was some measure of the general desire to disengage French colonialism entirely in the area. And so, as the French fought the Vietminh, they sought some sort of rear-guard diplomatic action with the other two countries and with the puppet regime of Bao Dai in Saigon. The recognition of this particular regime as an 'autonomous state' in 1949 raised logical questions about the nature of the French Union to which all three countries officially belonged in their capacity of 'Associated States'. In an effort at clarification and revision, the French government established a Ministry of the Associated States, an institutional, if not a practical, step in political devolution. The government also held a conference on the situation at Pau, France, between 29 June and 27 November 1950. Presided over by the very old but most durable Albert Sarraut, the conference consisted of representatives from Cambodia, Laos and Vietnam, as well as a contingent from France. The conference was largely a failure marked by suspicion, acrimony and growing disinclination at collaboration. The principal debate was over the structure of the

French Union, whether it should be an association of states under the aegis of France or an association of free peoples similar to the Commonwealth model. The conclusion was unsatisfactory but understandable. Each of the states now was granted internal autonomy, and a partnership in the settlement of federal issues, such as customs and finances. However, the end of the war and the realisation of the Geneva Accords allowed these states the same theoretical independence that Ho Chi Minh's Vietminh had acquired on the battlefield.

In 1954, Indochina was freed of French control. The dreadful futility of the war, its cost in lives, money, equipment and French morale cannot be estimated. The psychological cost can be measured personally and poignantly, however. As General de Lattre de Tassigny was beginning his new offensive in 1952, his only son, Bernard, an infantry lieutenant, was killed by enemy mortar fire. A striken and ill de Lattre left his command to accompany the body of his son home. What he brought back with that young corpse was the realisation of the futility of that war.

Yet this consideration was somehow forgotten or dismissed. Within a period of time slightly longer than three years, the French were to be involved in another colonial war, more intense, bitter and cruel than had been the one in Indochina.

7 Accumulating Failure: Morocco, Tunisia and Algeria

Interviewed for the July, 1956, issue of *Réalités*, the French Minister-Resident for Algeria, Robert Lacoste, remarked that the local population, considering that the French had suffered 'surrender following surrender', might have been led to believe that France would lose the struggle then being waged in Algeria. 'However, we held on', he laconically concluded.[1] For many years to come, until 1962 to be exact, the French continued to do that, in face of growing Muslim resistance, in response to itensifying settler determination, and in the hope of avoiding another outcome like that of Indochina.

Algeria was considered exceptional, unlike France's other colonial possessions. It was not in law an overseas possession, but an integral part of the republic, a salt-water extension of France itself. The popular slogan '*Algérie, c'est la France*' ('Algeria is France') was charged with emotion and highlighted by historical allusion. The first of France's acquisitions in empire building since the disastrous encounter of Montcalm and Fox on the Plains of Abraham in Quebec, Algeria was also the first and the largest of the three territories that were to comprise France's North African bloc of possessions.

North Africa was separated from France by a short sea distance and joined by a long military history. More romantic French historians might extend that reach back to King Louis XI and his Christian vocation which had brought him crusading to this region, first in 1248, when he was defeated and imprisoned in Egypt; then again in 1270, when he died in what became Tunisia. In point of political fact, however, the French first put foot firmly on North African soil after the military invasion of Algiers in 1830. Then, after a protectorate was established in Tunisia in 1881, the French added another with Morocco in 1912 and thus perfected colonial symmetry by the completion of their own variation of the 'Maghreb', the appealing definition earlier given to the northwestern province of the Ottoman Empire which had then embraced all of the territory now held by the French.

What the unfurled tricolour now shaded, the French imagination had already illuminated. This region, geographically defined by the blue Mediterranean and the white Sahara, was the essential part of the French 'Orient', an exceptional space of narrow, cluttered streets and vast desert emptiness that intrigued painters, poets, novelists and adventurers. Among that numerous company, perhaps the most popular, if neither real nor French, was the bar-keeper 'Rick' whom Humphrey Bogart so convincingly played in the 1942 film *Casablanca*. Now a major element in the study of film history, that American production stood apart from the some 200 films that the French themselves had produced between 1911 and 1962, films that followed the sweep of the camera across sparkling sand dunes and that inadequately framed the bazaars teeming with people and hung with brass pots and pans. Artfully, North Africa, more than any other part of the French overseas world, had been made an important part of the national landscape.

COLONIAL PROTEST IN FRENCH NORTH AFRICA

If falsely joined in foreign romance, the countries of the region were actually brought together in the spirit and act of revolt.[2] Geographic neighbours, sharing much of the same ecology which primarily made them pastoral peoples, profoundly influenced by Islam as a religion and a moral code, and certainly treated with a rude equality by the French who imposed their own language, laws and values, the populations of Morocco, Algeria and Tunisia, from west to east, remembered and were reminded of their distinctiveness.

These conditions of cultural identity and of commonalty of the political experience were expanded by events happening in other parts of the Muslim world. Since the collapse of the once politically embracing Ottoman Empire at the end of World War I, all of North Africa and the Near East was feverish and restless. Signs of hope and of inspiration appeared in the form of the new Republic of Turkey and in the British grant of formal independence to Egypt in 1922. During World War II, the end of the French mandates of Syria and Lebanon and the admission of Egypt to the United Nations as a charter member were reassuring to those who desired the end of empire. Then Libya's accession to nationhood in 1953 under United Nations supervision brought independence to the very borders of the French Maghreb.

Such developments were viewed anxiously by the French who were soon disturbed by the behaviour of Colonel Gamal A. Nasser, the new strongman in Egypt after the overthrow of the corrupt monarchy in 1952 and a most vocal partisan of North African independence. The French participation with the British in the invasion of Suez in 1956, joined to the war then being waged between Israel and Egypt, was in response to Nasser's seizure of the canal. However, the French involvement was in large measure conditioned by the concern, later proved false, that Nasser was lending support to the Algerians in their war against France. Confronted by Russian threats and American remonstrances, the expeditionary force left nearly as quickly as it came. The Suez incident thus became the last, perhaps most futile, act of old-fashioned imperialism during which Union Jack and Tricolour snapped briskly in a favourable wind.[3]

In these new regional circumstances of cultural unity and political disarray, the growth of a spirit of dissent from and resistance to French colonial rule was here more intense than in most other parts of that nation's colonial empire. While the official policy of pacification – military investment of the country – continued well into the twentieth century, the most pronounced developments in the inter-war period were responses to cultural change, to what the French modified of the old, to what the French denied of the new. The first was a direct consequence of reform, of the French tendency to interfere with old customs and institutions, most of which had a religious basis. The second was generated by the friction of exclusion, the denial to North Africans of those political rights and practices that the French advertised abroad as the hallmark of France since the Revolution of 1789. In defending the old and in demanding the new, the North African colonial elite seized upon the instruments that the French themselves had imported as they settled in: the press, the political party, the trade union and the strike being the most obvious.

Even before World War II had brutally destroyed the old global order of things, dissent was widely registered in North Africa. Among those eruptions which disturbed but did not yet flaw the colonial structure, a few are of such proportions that they merit attention. In Morocco, the promulgation in 1930 of a *dahir*, or royal law, designed to modernise the legal system and bring it more under French control, was an actual denial of the authority of the traditional Berber courts, operating on Islamic religious principles. Thus about three-fifths of the population was effectively removed from the sultan's jurisdiction, an act perceived as an infringement of Moroccan sovereignty and an act which was described in *Morocco*, a pamphlet published by the Istiqlal Party in 1955, as marking 'the starting point of the new form taken by the Moroccan Nationalist Movement'.[4]

Shortly after the expression of popular resentment over the *dahir*, a new political movement was gaining widespread support in Tunisia.[5] Under the able leadership of Habib Bourguiba, then a dynamic lawyer and forceful journalist, the Neo-Destour Party was established in 1934, a more advanced political outgrowth of the Destour Party that had been established in 1920. Bourguiba's activism disturbed the French authorities who responded in what was already the classic colonial response: a jail sentence. Released in 1936, he set about making the Neo-Destour a mass party. The Neo-Destour, in collaboration with the General Confederation of Tunisian Labour (the CGTT), itself an offshoot of the chief French labour union, began a major strike in 1938 in protest against the firing of an Algerian worker in the city of Bizerte. Widespread and large-scaled demonstrations now occurred, these fuelled by the arrest of Bourguiba once again and by the temporary outlawing of the Neo-Destour Party. On 9 April 1938, a large crowd converged in Tunis to protest against these actions; French troops fired on the crowd with the resultant loss of 122 lives.

Nothing so violent happened in Algeria at this time, except at the end of the era, in that moment of celebration of the victory in Europe over Nazi Germany. Then there was an uprising and riot in Sétif, an essentially Muslim town, west of Constantine and beyond the mainstream of French colonial activities. On 8 May, as the French gathered together in the town square to begin their celebration of the European peace achieved on V-E Day, a group of Muslims, carrying revolutionary banners and moving angrily forward, struck out at the crowd.

What precipitated this uprising and exactly how it began are still matters of debate. However, it is certain that the mob was spurred on by economic deprivation as well as the desire for colonial reform.

During the next five days, as the helpless French were assailed, the violence to person and to property was horrible. Then French troops finally arrived and the bloody tide swept the other way. This bidirectional frenzy whipped up lasting anger and animosity – some consider the events of Sétif the awakening of an Algerian national spirit of independence – and left behind an appalling, if ill-determined number of dead, between 1000 and 6000 persons.

Although the officially described 'incident' was played down by the French press, in a euphoric state over the defeat of Nazi Germany, the violence at Sétif does seem in retrospect to be the tragic beginning of the end, of that brutal dialectic of militant protest and military response that was the condition of colonialism in Algeria for the next two decades.

Yet, in 1945, the French quickly restored order and therefore assumed that they could right matters to their satisfaction once they had returned to full authority in Algeria.

THE END OF COLONIAL RULE IN MOROCCO AND TUNISIA

As if obeying some unpromulgated historical law, the three North African countries pulled away from French rule in reverse order to their political absorption. The reasons are clear. First, the relatively long period of French intrusion into and then settlement of Algeria created a more deeply seated French power which was greatly reinforced, in large measure determined, by the resident European population which adamantly resisted any change that threatened their privileged position. The settlers in Morocco and Tunisia were fewer in number and more concentrated in the cities and the professions. Second, the French modes of colonial rule had been modified as the two more recent possessions had been acquired. Tunisia and Morocco had rather effective indigenous governments which the French left in place and which they supervised by a system of indirect rule, under the aegis of a 'resident' not a 'governor'. Thus, nothing like the political and bureaucratic assimilation of Algeria to France was found in the two protectorates. Third, and largely as a result of the preceding two conditions, neither Tunisia nor Morocco was so emotionally charged as a French national issue, so clearly seen as integral to French political well-being.

A final element has to do with the nature of the forces opposing France: in both Morocco and Tunisia, there was a leader around which the population could rally. In Morocco, it was the sultan; in Tunisia, it was Bourguiba, who later acquired the less than beguiling title of 'Supreme Warrior'. In Algeria, on the contrary, the older and more contentious leadership of Ferhat Abbas and Messali Hadj was not resolved into a single focal point of national direction. When the National Liberation Front (the FLN) became a political force in 1954, it turned away from these men and established a policy of rule by committee.

Although the nationalist movement in Tunisia was older and more advanced than that in Morocco, the latter country gained independence first. As good a date as any by which to mark the commencement of the end of French rule in Morocco is 1943, when a meeting between the Sultan of Morocco, Mohammed Ben Yousef, and President Franklin D. Roosevelt took place, during the Casablanca Conference which was held in January. Although the French protested this initiative, which had the appearance of one head of state meeting another, Roosevelt proceeded as he wished and even discussed Moroccan independence, although his exact words are disputed.

The spirit of the meeting buoyed nationalist Moroccan politicians. A year later, on 11 January 1944, the Istiqlal Party proclaimed its existence in a manifesto which requested that the sultan seek the nation's independence. The party grew rapidly, becoming a dominant political force as it called for a constitutional monarchy as well as the right to national sovereignty.[6] Moreover, the party established a special rapport with the sultan who, however, remained officially above the strife until a more dramatic and central role was forced upon him.

By 1953 the French had taken draconian measures in the light of intensifying urban riots. The Istiqlal Party had already been outlawed, and now the sultan was deposed and exiled to Madagascar, the French arguing the need for this move as they feared for the ruler's safety. Nothing was achieved, other than the generation of strong public support for the politically sacrificed sultan. Disorder spread as Moroccans protested the French action and as a group of resident French, styling themselves the French Presence (*Présence française*), determined to make that particular presence known. In a countermove to a bombing that occurred in Casablanca in 1955, the

French Presence took matters into its own hands by moving into the Moroccan zone of the city, then destroying property and killing several Moroccans. This general social deterioration, which threatened anarchy, was a condition that the French government could not sustain, giving the taxing problems with which it was confronted in Algeria and given the on-going effort it was then making to negotiate a final settlement with Tunisia.

Quickly, the sultan was returned by the French, an occasion on which the ruler was greeted as a national hero. But before his triumphal entrance, the cause he now espoused had triumphed: the French signed with him an agreement on 6 November 1955, announcing the end of the protectorate. That final action officially took place on 2 March 1956.

Tunisia followed in political success, this country perhaps the best prepared of the French colonial possessions to assume independence. The Neo-Destour Party was the centre of the nationalist activity, and Bourguiba was both its enlightened and unswerving leader. Arrested twice before, Bourguiba spent much time in exile during World War II and then spent further time abroad as an emissary of his nation seeking help for its cause.

Bourguiba attempted to galvanise world opinion, and in large measure he succeeded. No doubt this favourable development was greatly due to his pragmatism. What would later be called 'Bourguibism' was a form of political gradualism, the effort to take advantage of every opportunity and of every negotiation to achieve the end of national independence. Opponents often called this tactic collaboration with the enemy – Bourguiba was even labelled a 'fascist' – but steadfast determination and clear vision kept him moving forward.

Already in 1945, Bourguiba issued a manifesto claiming independence, even though he knew at the time that there was no hope for such an outcome. The French ignored the manifesto but did initiate limited political reform in order to relieve the tense conditions in the country. Temporising, the French devised the principle of 'co-sovereignty' whereby representation on the Grand Council, the chief parliamentary body, remained equally divided between French and Tunisians, while an increase in the number of Tunisians in the administration was admitted. These modest actions, taken in 1951, followed shortly upon a speech by the French foreign minister, Robert Schumann, in which he had actually spoken of Tunisian independence. Thus what occurred in the form of change did not match what had been said, a further inconsistency in French policy and a further aggravation to the Tunisians.

The next major French move was the appointment of Jean de Hautecloque as resident-general. This brusque military figure initiated a repressive policy having as its objective the brisk reassertion of French authority and the halting of strikes and other methods of protest. In late January 1952, Hautecloque sent troops into the region of Cape Bon, just south of Tunis, where they pillaged and brutally treated the indigenous population. Matters only got worse in that year with the murder of several nationalist leaders including the head of the UGTT.

The local turmoil was matched by French confusion at home and elsewhere abroad. As short-lived governments attempted to cope with European issues such as re-armament, the United Nations was the scene of debates over French Tunisian policy, and Indochina remained the place of unresolved military engagement. About the only positive action the national government took in Tunisia was the recall of Hautecloque and, consequently, the easing of the repressive measures he had imposed.

If there was a dramatic turn of events, however, it occurred when Pierre Mendès-France became premier on 19 June 1954, and brought to that office unusual resolve and equally unusual clear vision. Mendès-France was determined to settle the worst problems abroad, those of Indochina and North Africa. He prepared for the Geneva Conference, and then turned his attention directly to Tunisia. On 31 July 1954, in the company of the staid General Alphonse Juin, he went to Tunisia where he issued the 'Declaration of Carthage' in which he recognised the principle of Tunisian independence and proposed the preparation of a set of agreements to assure it. The French in Tunisia were unsettled by this swift decision but were now unable to do much about it because they could find little support at home. The National Assembly had now focused its concern elsewhere, on the deteriorating situation in Algeria, which was reason enough to resolve the political problem in Tunisia immediately.

Accordingly, the French government allowed Bourguiba, under arrest in France since 1955, to return to Tunisia on 1 June 1957. Then on 3 June, after much public rejoicing, France signed with Tunisia six conventions which established self-government and which regulated a series of economic, social and cultural matters concerning French nationals in Tunisia as well as the French government. The last act occurred on 20 March 1958, when a Protocol of Agreement was concluded giving Tunisia 'full sovereignty'.

Thus, the French withdrew from two-thirds of their North African possessions, yet this still left without solution the future condition of the last third, by far the biggest region, the place of the most difficult political problems, the setting of the deepest animosity.

THE WAR IN ALGERIA

Algeria was a place apart, even though considered an integral part of France.[7] It was in effect, if not in official terminology, a settlement colony, with approximately one-eighth of its population (some 1 250 000 out of 9 000 000) being of European origin, chiefly French and Italian. While the French-designed cityscape spread gracefully along the coast, the rural landscape was starkly colonial, dominated by the large farms occupied by the *pieds noirs*, so-called because of the inexpensive black shoes many of them wore. In *The Wretched of the Earth*, Frantz Fanon singles out the settler as the chief enemy of the Algerian people, the chief creator of the colonial situation. The settler had appropriated the land, Fanon asserted, thus displacing the *fellahs*, peasants whose existence had been landbased and backbent for centuries on end. It was for this reason that Fanon insisted that the *fellah*'s nationalism was felt between his toes.[8]

The resident European minority of colonial city dwellers and farmers working the land was a political and social majority, largely controlling Algerian affairs and enjoying a privileged position in the French parliamentary system because Algeria had been made an integral part of the republic and accordingly divided into three departments which were separated from the vast and sparsely settled 'Territory of the South' where the Algerian nomadic way of life persisted and where the French ruled in a pronounced colonial manner.

So entrenched in Algeria and protected by a powerful political lobby in Paris, the European Algerians lived in a special light. No French politican could afford to make a public statement that did not support the tired contention that Algeria was a part of France. Even Pierre Mendès-France, as liberal and as enlightened as anyone involved with decolonisation, remarked, in a speech given on 12

November 1964, less than two weeks after the FLN declaration of independence, that the Algerian departments are 'irrevocably French'. This insistence on distinguishing Algeria from the rest of *France d'Outre-Mer* made any accommodation with Algerian protestors a difficult posture to assume. That difficulty was intensified by the still sorely-felt emotions generated by the French defeat at Dien Bien Phu. The military, as well as many politicians, were determined that no such humiliation would occur in Algeria.

These briefly described sentiments swirled around the Algerian landscape, beclouding it. Nothing was cleared up or cleared away until the Fourth Republic itself was swept away by the fire storm in Algeria, and General de Gaulle then assumed political authority at home.[9] Yet when the Algerian War began in the early morning of All Saint's Day, 1 November 1954, its occurrence was immediately dismissed as another easily contained uprising. The French had some reason to believe so.

Well-planned and widely executed, the attack was nevertheless largely unsuccessful, neither causing severe damage nor arousing much fervour among Algerian Muslims. The proclamation of the newly defined National Liberation Front was, however, grand in statement, uncompromising in principle: national independence to be reached by whatever means necessary. Although the proclamation proposed 'an honorable platform for the discussion with French authorities', it prefaced this statement with one of determination: 'the struggle will be long, but the outcome is certain...'.

The French chose to ignore this statement, as they had ignored so many others, because its conditions were unacceptable. Nevertheless, French intelligence had already been made aware of and was properly impressed by the careful and effective means of organisation that the FLN had already achieved. After years of political dissension and personality conflict, a younger group within the Movement for the Triumph of Democratic Liberties (the MTLD), which was the latest denomination of Messali Hadj's party, begun in the 1930s as the North African Star, created an underground militant arm, the Special Organisation (OS), which began training a cadre for guerrilla warfare. Discovered and destroyed by the French, the Special Organisation had already enlisted some 1500 members, among which a determined leadership that now formed the Revolutionary Committee for Action and Unity (CRUA) in 1954, and, following news of the French defeat at Dien Bien Phu, prepared to act. It was this group that designed the 1 November 1954 uprising and, in turn, created the FLN.

Whether France could have prevented or prohibited independence is most doubtful, but the success of the FLN and its fighting arm, the ALN (National Liberation Army), would not have been so quickly pronounced if the French had carried through meaningful reform rather than pasting together the old in slightly different arrangements.

In 1946 the French government had approved the Statute for Algeria which offered some political modification. The country would have greater internal autonomy provided by a general assembly elected through two colleges: one for French citizens, the other for Muslims. The demographic disparity that the system legalised (equal seats for the two populations in which the French citizenry were a decided minority) was further reinforced by the political authority of the governor-general to impose a two-thirds vote, instead of a majority vote, on any matter he chose, thus blocking the possibility of legislation or policy unfavourable to French interests. Some recognition of Algerian cultural identity was made by the separation of the Muslim religion from the state and by the allowance of Arabic as a language of instruction. Nevertheless, these reforms were not implemented, and the elections to the assembly were notoriously rigged. The Statute for Algeria thus mocked the Algerians and was soon mocked by those demanding independence.

More significantly, the French failure to provide meaningful reform undermined the reform movements which had been created within the Algerian population. Ferhat Abbas was finally persuaded to throw in his lot with the FLN in 1956. Shortly thereafter, he was elected a member of the National Council of the Algerian Revolution (CNRA), the governing body of the FLN, and then became premier of the Provisional Government of the Republic of Algeria (GPRA) in 1958. In changing his position, Abbas recognised, as he concluded in his retrospective study, that 'the era of broken promises was gone forever'.[10]

THE NATURE AND INTENSITY OF THE COLONIAL WAR

The war in Algeria was the most brutal of the colonial struggles, even though – perhaps because – the vast number of conscripts was given policing responsibilities and the task of actual fighting was primarily that assigned to the professional units.[11] The defiguring of French victims, the widespread appearance of *le grand sourire* ('the broad smile'), as the French macabrely described the Algerian practice of throat slitting, the bombing of civilian public places – these acts of terrorism aroused a comparable response. French soldiers began the practice of torture to obtain information and engaged in indiscriminate killing that shocked the population at home. French intellectuals vigorously protested these practices, seeing that the very soul of the nation was threatened.[12] French soldiers occasionally shivered at the thought that their behaviour was not dissimilar to that of the Nazis in Occupied France. The war was thus dispiriting and disturbing, moods deepened by the lack of clearly defined military objectives, by the lack of political plan and resolve. Never recognised by the French government as a war – for which reason the famous *Croix de Guerre* was not awarded – the struggle went on for seven years.

It began, the enormity and brutality of it, all at once, in the resort town of Philippeville in the oppressive heat of August, 1955. Until this time, in the eight months since the FLN had declared its intention of independence, the ALN had engaged in a series of disruptive forays, principally against military strongpoints and for the purpose of harrassment of French troops and the seizure of arms. The FLN was therefore perceived by the French as being more a nuisance than a serious threat.

Furthermore, the intelligent plan devised by the new governor-general, Jacques Soustelle, a former university professor and a liberal supporter of General de Gaulle during the war, held promise of success. Arriving in Algiers in February 1955, Soustelle proposed a policy of 'integration', a more liberal form of association, in which Algerian interests would be both respected and enhanced; and he developed a new agency, the Special Administrative Service (SAS), composed of well-trained French officers who could serve in the Algerian countryside as advisers, technicians, aides – in short as technicians and consultants to the local populations.

The liberal inclination of Soustelle, which immediately generated severe antagonism among the *pieds noirs*, was sharply altered in but a few months, perhaps during his inspection tour that followed quickly upon the massacre at Philippeville. The decision to attack the civilian population of that city, to create a scene of brutal destruction and dreadful carnage, hence to force the French to counter with a military commitment that would thereupon generate further support for the FLN among the still hesitant population, was a calculated element of guerrilla warfare. It was the decision reached by the leadership of Wilaya 2, one of the six such military divisions by which the FLN organised the country.

Highly compartmentalised, constructed rather like a series of clusters forming a pyramid, FLN organisation was designed to assure that no more than a handful of members ever knew one another, a precaution against infiltration and destruction. Wilaya 2 was the strongest of these major military districts in 1955 and, fearful that the revolutionary movement would slow down, determined that dramatic and dreadful action was required. On 20 August 1955, the FLN struck Philippeville. The loss of life was appalling, with the incensed French responding in a cycle of violence that matched the barbarism of the FLN. What Soustelle saw among the dead and the wounded that he visited was a condition he could not have previously imagined. Liberal policy vanished from his new vision of things, as it did from the vision of all the French who had witnessed or read about the massacre.

Colonial rule now gave way to aggressive war.

'Colonialism', Frantz Fanon would later write, 'is violence in its natural state, and it will only yield when confronted with greater violence.'[13] These words derive in part from Fanon's experience as a medical doctor with the FLN, but they clearly express the conditions that developed in Algeria after 1955. As terrorism intensified, the French military effort was drastically altered. Men – ultimately half a million – and equipment – helicopters assuming a new military role there – were rushed in, while military strategy was reworked, the experience in Indochina now translated to new ground. Highly mobile combat teams combed the countryside for FLN guerrillas while a policy of population relocation was instituted to assure surveillance and to isolate groups from infiltration by the FLN.

However, the major military development, a resounding French success and an FLN blunder was 'The Battle of Algiers' which occurred early in 1957. General Jacques Massu, commander of the 10th Paratroop Division, was given an order by the resident-minister, Robert Lacoste, to thwart a planned labour strike in the city and to clear the city of the FLN. The strike was arranged to coincide with the opening of the General Assembly of the United Nations and thereby to attract world attention to the Algerian cause.

The city of Algiers was silent and calm that morning of 28 January, as Algerians stayed home. Massu's troops entered the city, pulled down the shutters of the closed shops and forced the shopkeepers to open up. They then proceeded to search the city quarter-by-quarter and succeeded in destroying the FLN hideouts by obtaining information through the device of torture.[14]

The battle was quickly won, but it was a defeat for the civilian leadership in Algiers and for the government in Paris, both of which had in effect turned over control of the war and of Algeria to the military. Henceforth, a tense relationship developed between the government in Paris and the army in Algeria, while the army and the *pieds noirs*, never on good terms, did at least agree on the need for brute force. As the army succeeded militarily, the FLN grew stronger politically, and the general colonial situation deteriorated steadily.

Then, a series of acts threatened the integrity of the French government itself and, finally, precipitated the fall of that government.

REVOLT AGAINST PARIS

The chief development of the war was distrust: the *pieds noirs* feared a negotiated peace with the FLN, the army was concerned about the weakness of the government and its wavering resolve to assure a military solution, while the government was disturbed by the possibility of unbridled military action. Algeria may have been France, to borrow the popular slogan, but the multiple divisions in it and between it and Paris denied any sense of unity of purpose, save the need to end the war favourably.

In desperation and out of frustration, the *pieds noirs*, appalled at the weakness and the hesitancy of the successive governments of the Fourth Republic, moved to revolutionary action of their own. The precipitant was the proposed creation of a new government under Pierre Pflimlin which was to include none of the known sympathisers with the *pieds noirs*, a governmental development occurring just after the FLN execution of three French soldiers.

Calling for a general strike and a memorial service, both as an expression of discontent with the government and of solidarity with the army, the leadership of the *pieds noirs* led a huge crowd to the main government building in Algiers, seized it while the army watched and declared on that morning of 13 May 1958, the establishment of a Committee of Public Safety which General Jacques Massu was asked to head. Massu later said that he had accepted the position only to prevent further disturbances, but his action indicated that the army had now joined with the settlers in open defiance of the government in Paris.

A week of agitation and confusion ensued as the newly installed Pflimlin government tried to prepare for the worst, which now included 'Operation Resurrection', a planned assault by the army in Algeria on Paris, purportedly to install a provisional government under Charles de Gaulle. In the meanwhile, de Gaulle assumed a delphic attitude and spoke in terms that pleased no group and offended no other. However, when General Raoul Salan, commander-in chief of the French military forces in Algeria, added a loud 'Vive de Gaulle!' as a sort of afterthought to a speech he made on 15 May to a large crowd in Algiers, de Gaulle quickly and publicly responded by stating that he was ready to assume power.

Days of confusion again followed, with the threat of military action against the government given further credence with the seizure of Corsica by a contingent of paratroopers. Tanks were now swiftly rolled into Paris as the political talks slowly rolled on. Finally, on 1 June 1958, the French National Assembly voted to install Charles de Gaulle as premier. This act, the last of the series in which Algiers had indirectly ruled Paris for years, was the first scene of the denouement of the Algerian drama in which de Gaulle played an essential, if enigmatic, role.

DE GAULLE'S ALGERIAN POLICY

If there is an irony found in the next phase of the war, it is in the coincidence of an opportunity for French military success and de Gaulle's conclusion that a negotiated withdrawal was the only lasting solution available. About de Gaulle's analysis of the Algerian situation much controversy has been generated, in part because he remained 'the General', a person of a haughty demeanour that seemed of the same measurement as his height, and of obscure intention that seemed only to unfold with the same slow cadence as the delivery of his television addresses.

Recognising the possibility of another 13 May protest, de Gaulle moved quickly to reorganise the Algerian military command, now placing its leadership in the hands of General Maurice Challe, an able air force general who vigorously set upon the task of destroying the National Liberation Army. With the effective use of helicopters, the most innovative aspect of the technology of the Algerian War, and through the tactical movement of small-scale combat teams that sought to destroy their ALN counterparts, Challe pushed the enemy back and swept away much of the accumulated hope of the FLN leadership. Under these favourable circumstances, Challe thought he could win decisively on the battlefield, but de Gaulle's attention was directed elsewhere for the best solution.

Those who had elected Charles de Gaulle as president, following the promulgation of the constitution of the Fifth Republic on 4 October 1958, were largely in agreement that negotiations over Algeria's status should only follow the achievement of French military advantage, and that negotiation should not lead to independence. Those, chiefly among the *pieds noirs*, who wished the *status quo ante bellum* were supporting what de Gaulle derisively referred to as the *Algérie du papa*. Those of more liberal persuasion assumed that Algeria should be modernised and given greater autonomy under French supervision, preferably through a meaningful policy of integration. Germaine Tillion, one of the most intelligent and knowledgeable observers of Algeria and at one time adviser to Jacques Soustelle wrote in her fascinating book *France and Algeria*: 'Frenchmen and Algerians – it is impossible to conceive of two populations whose mutual dependence is more certain'.[15] That particular assertion seemed all the more compelling with the discovery of oil in the Algerian Sahara and with it the promise of both the energy and the capital necessary to modernise Algeria.

Still immediately hopeful of the still uncertain future, the French people awaited de Gaulle's initiative. It turned out to be not what most had expected with certainty.

De Gaulle's rhetoric swung away from *Algérie française*, but only after he had turned around local conditions to where he was well positioned politically. In 1958, local elections increased the number of positions held by Algerian Muslims. In October of the same year, de Gaulle announced the Constantine Plan, in the city of that name,

which was a modernisation plan of previously unimaginable proportions that, in two years, led to impressive works projects, public
housing and pipeline construction, and financial support for schools.

De Gaulle now began to speak of the 'Algerian personality', a
concept both ambiguous and suggestive, a metaphorical shift in the
direction of the political position he announced in a major broadcast
of 16 September 1959. The Algerian problem, he announced on that
occasion, will not be solved 'by tossing at each other empty and
oversimplified slogans'. Then he proposed three alternatives to the
Algerian people, to be allowed only after the restoration of peace:
secession, 'out-and-out identification with France' (integration) or
a federal relationship in which France would provide assistance with
the economy and education and direction in matters of defence and
foreign affairs.

This disavowal of *Algérie française*, this suggestion that the
'Algerian personality' could be modified or entirely remoulded, was
disturbing to the French in Algeria and disquieting to the military
which still expected victory on the battlefield.

THE MILITARY MALCONTENTS

In the sequence of major events that disturbed the Algerian scene
in these years, the next were expressions of acute dissatisfaction
among the 'ultras' and the military in and out of the country.
Everywhere in Algeria among the French a sort of colonial xeno-
phobia seeped upward, a growing distrust of de Gaulle's intentions,
a fear of possible betrayal of the cause of *Algérie française*, a
suspected disregard of the long French tradition in the country and
of the special place carved out by many, not least of which was the
Foreign Legion.

This attitude was converted into hastily contrived structures on
24 January 1960, the beginning of what has since been called 'The
Week of the Barricades'. Barricades were erected by the 'ultras' in
central Algiers and the guard units which were sent in to pull them
down were greeted with gunfire. The guards quickly retreated,
leaving behind fourteen dead, this while the army, within earshot of
the fracas, remained disengaged. For the remainder of the week
hesitancy and confusion reigned, in no way relieved by the depar-

ture of General Challe from the city, he seeking to remove himself from proximity to culpability or support. On 29 January de Gaulle again appeared on the television screen and in a moving speech first declared that 'the Algerians shall have free choice of their destiny' and then reminded the army that the war was 'France's war' and that 'in your mission there is no room for equivocation or interpretation'.

The work of the barricaders, along with their hope, quickly fell when the army was no longer involved. Chagrin was heavy in the air, however. As General de Gaulle proceeded along his ill-defined path to peace, the army leaders who had served in Algeria and had sided with the cause of the French residents grew more bitter. Their sentiments were corroded into a bond of conspiracy after de Gaulle made another of his television speeches, the important one of 4 November 1960, in which he stated that the new course he had followed since his return to the presidency now 'leads not to an Algeria governed by Metropolitan France but to an Algerian Algeria. This means an emancipated Algeria in which the Algerians themselves will decide their destiny...'.[16]

This speech stood as a prefatory statement to a referendum announced to be held on 6 January 1961, which would serve as a popular indication of support for de Gaulle's policy and for his position as guide through the morass which was the situation in Algeria. The French voted overwhelmingly in favour of de Gaulle's position, an outcome that only further displeased the already discontented in Algiers and also those cast from that local scene, those generals whom de Gaulle had earlier reposted because of the support of the *pieds noirs*.

The next outburst of protest occurred on 22 April, when the First Foreign Paratroop Regiment seized control of Algiers. This action, to which several other military groups rallied, was the handiwork of a number of discontented colonels who had perceived the army once again being used and discarded, rather like a shell casing, by the civilian government. Gaining the support of the then-retired General Challe and also confronted with the unanticipated assistance of General Salan, refuged in Spain, the conspiring colonels prepared an ill-defined coup d'état. Salan dreamed of overthrowing de Gaulle; Challe hoped to hand the general a decisive military victory that he could not refuse – or so he said after the failure of the coup.

Once again, de Gaulle aired his distress and disgust, the broadcast reaching the soldiers in Algeria on transistor radios. Whether his words or the already perceived foolishness of the enterprise caused the army to deny the support Challe required, the military conspiracy failed and with it any attempt at forceful change of national policy. Now the 'ultras' went underground, formed the Secret Army Organisation (OAS) which, until peace was negotiated, harrassed and destroyed and thus unintentionally won further support for de Gaulle's policy.

Soon engaging in selective assassination in Algeria, the OAS also turned to France in late 1961 where bombings occurred along with an attempted assassination of Charles de Gaulle and an intended dynamiting of the Eiffel Tower. It was the wanton bombing of the home of the Minister of Culture, André Malraux, which resulted in the dreadful disfiguring of a four-year-old child that turned French opinion against the OAS and away from the Algerian cause. Like their president, the French people were now anxious to be done with the problems of *Algérie française*.

TOWARD ALGERIAN PEACE AND FRENCH WITHDRAWAL

It was the spa city of Evian that was the centre of negotiations between leaders of the FLN and members of the French government. The first round of talks, which had lasted for several weeks between May and July of 1961, ended in failure. Suspicion and obduracy were the reasons, both sides entangled in a series of events and problems of unusual complexity. One such event should alone indicate the intensity of the difficulties. This was the famous Ben Bella affair.

One of the major leaders of the FLN, Ben Bella, and three other leaders, had been invited as guests of the king of Morocco to discuss the Algerian situation. Returning to their temporary headquarters in Tunis aboard a Moroccan airliner flown by a French pilot, they were diverted to Algiers where, upon landing, they were arrested by the French military. This aerial hijacking had occurred on 22 October 1956, and to the surprise of the Guy Mollet government in France, which had been uninvolved. Unable to disavow the act by releasing Ben Bella for fear of outbursts of displeasure among the *pieds noirs*, the government jailed the Algerians in France. The FLN insisted upon the release of Ben Bella; indeed the Provisional Government of the Republic of Algeria wanted him to be one of its negotiators at Evian. The French, considering Ben Bella a conspirator and yet now recognising the provisional government, balked at the suggestion. Ben Bella was excluded, but the French made him accessible to the FLN leadership.

The second round of talks, begun on 7 March 1962, concluded successfully on 18 March, with agreement that a cease-fire would be implemented the following day and with peace arrangements that were satisfactory to both sides. The accords also satisfied the rhetoric that had been generated on both sides by providing for a transitional period in which a French High Commissioner would exercise French legal authority while sovereignty was in fact transferred to the Algerians through a provisional executive, including both Algerians and French residents. This provisional executive was to prepare a plebiscite which would determine the definitive form of government.

Other conditions also bore the mark of compromise. The French residents could retain their current status for three years and then become Algerian citizens, should they so choose. The oil of the Sahara, the disposition of which had been a perplexing issue, was to be jointly exploited by the French and the Algerians. And of final consequence, the French would retain Mers-el-Kebir as a naval base for a minimum of fifteen years, with the possibility of renewal of this treaty provision.

Algeria became a sovereign state on 1 July 1962.

THE COLONIAL SIGNIFICANCE OF ALGERIA

The tortuous disengagement from Algeria was actually the last major act of French decolonisation. By the time of Algerian independence, the colonies in West and Equatorial Africa had become nations. There is thus something of an overarching irony in the historical realisation that modern French colonial history begins and ends with Algeria, begins and ends with military encounter there. That irony is sharpened by the realisation that the geographical antipodes of French colonial empire – Algeria and Indochina – were similar extremes, the locations of the two most serious wars of decolonisation.

Never did the Empire look so good as when it was seen from the Republic, it was said of Napoleon III's regime in the early years of the Third Republic. With slight modification, the statement might also stand for the French vision of Indochina and Algeria right after World War II.

8 The Peaceful Devolution of Authority: Sub-Saharan Africa

One of the most famous of children's stories is Antoine de Saint-Exupéry's *The Little Prince*, a whimsical account of a little boy from a far-away asteroid who happens into the Sahara Desert, where the stranded author encounters him. Saint-Exupéry was there, both in fact and fiction, as an airline pilot delivering mail for the Latocère air service that maintained a regular, if frequently disrupted, service between Toulouse, France and Dakar, Senegal, in the interwar period. Saint-Exupéry's story emerges from one of the occasions of motor failure that he endured and as he waited in the desert for a relief plane.

This aerial connection was the most recent of the several means by which the French had maintained contact with West Africa since the time Dieppe fishing ships had first arrived off the coast in the sixteenth century. While not painted in exotic colours as was North Africa, and while not regarded with the awe that were the cultures of Indochina, the land and the people described as Black Africa inspired a rich travel literature and added to European artistic innovation when Pablo Picasso and others found in African sculpture the configurations that were to help shape Cubism.

A long tradition of cultural contact with the region was brightly embroidered by the French with commentary on the success of their colonial policy, informed by the idea of assimilation. This vast region of Black Africa dominated by the French was therefore given a special place in the annals of French colonialism as the primeval scene of soulful encounter, the setting of brotherhood formed by the land itself. French West Africa allowed 'the religious return of man to the land, of man to man', wrote Robert Delavignette in the first pages of his book *Afrique occidentale française*, commissioned as part of the 1931 International Colonial Exposition.[1]

If history were composed of homilies, the writer of French imperialism might say that it was fitting that France's Sub-Saharan colonies should be among the last to be given up and done so with

115

some grace, certainly with no severe violence and with little anguish expressed by either side.

THE FRENCH INVOLVEMENT IN BLACK AFRICA

Despite their long-extending interest in Sub-Saharan Africa, the French were never as intensely involved there as they were elsewhere.[2] The region seemed neither to offer the economic promise of others nor to enter French thought regularly when global strategy was considered. Moreover, while the French population was not easily attracted to settlement in any part of the colonial empire, Sub-Saharan Africa was the least appealing part. It thus remained principally a set of places in which administrative activity prevailed more than did commercial affairs or plantation development. As proof of this assertion, one need only examine the demographic statistics: among a population of some 23 000 000 Africans living in French West Africa just before World War II, there were only 90 000 Frenchmen, administrators included.

This peripheral location on the wide circle of colonial affairs was further accentuated during World War II when the region formed the one principal set of French territories not seriously intruded upon by military activity. Thus, although the dispute between the authority of the Vichy government and that of the Free French under General de Gaulle was disruptive, the wartime experience caused no direct significant change in colonial status. Even the Brazzaville Conference, as has been noted, reflected old attitudes more than new visions.

If Sub-Saharan Africa was seldom pressing in French colonial affairs, local conditions do explain the final ease of transition to nationhood, the lack of strident rhetoric and the absence of military engagement that had occurred in Africa north of the desert. First, the colonies south of the Sahara were essentially French creations, their boundaries determined by Europeans rather than by pre-existing ethnic considerations or earlier-established political systems. Generally small-scale in form, the pre-colonial African governing authority was further restricted in size by a multiplicity of local languages and often rather difficult conditions of transportation and communication. Only occasionally by military force was a large state, a local empire, created, as in the most famous instance, that of Samory in the middle of the nineteenth century, an empire against which the French fought long and hard.

The demographic situation formed another factor of major importance. Given the fact that the population was thinly distributed over agriculturally poor land, the French colonial system was never very imposing in structure, often represented only by the colonial commandant on horse, or later in car, making a grand circuit that touched, but did not gravely disturb or profoundly influence, the people encountered. This limited and widely dispersed population partially explains why the French practices of forced labour and, later, military recruitment in World War I were greeted with such antagonism and violent protest.

Of equal significance in any balancing of colonial accounts is the nature of French colonial rule in West Africa. The territorial acquisitions were primarily made in the nineteenth century by military explorations and expeditions which resulted in a military form of colonial organisation, the basic administrative unit being the military *cercle*. In Equatorial Africa an earlier experiment with chartered companies, having, as did those in some of the British East African possessions, both commercial advantage and the responsibility to govern, was soon abandoned. Although the region was then submitted to civilian control, it remained in every way behind West Africa in terms of colonial consideration and development.

Thus, unlike the British in their neighbouring African colonies, where civilian rule was the norm and where consultative assemblies had been established by the early twentieth century, the French introduced little that prepared the indigenous populations for representative government. The one exception was geographically limited. In the 'Four Old Communes' of Senegal (the towns of St Louis, Dakar, Rufisque and the island of Gorée) residents enjoyed the political privileges of French towns and had, since 1848, elected a representative to the French parliament. In 1912 that position was won in a hotly contested election by Blaise Diagne, the first Black African to sit in the Chamber of Deputies in Paris. The right to vote was extended after World War I to certain veterans, but over most of the vast African territories the population was treated as culturally inferior, thus politically subordinate.

Added together, these conditions marked the nature of French colonial rule and determined its degree of success in this part of the world. As the postwar world opened, the results were unimpressive: insignificant social formation (literacy reached only 11% in 1946), small-scale trade, uninspiring urban development. The colonial environment was variously described as sleepy in mood or small-town Provençal in appearance, with the French population languishing from little to do. As for the one major city that did arise in the early twentieth century to serve both as port of commerce and naval station, Dakar in Senegal, it inspired little praise. One interwar visitor commented of Dakar that '. . . only one word comes to mind with which to qualify all that man has done here: mediocrity'.[3]

Far-removed in the French imagination and far-ranging in the French administrative perception, the territories south of the Sahara under French rule were organised in the early twentieth century into two vast federations, French West Africa and French Equatorial Africa, with a governor-general seated in Dakar for the one and in Brazzaville for the other.

Attractive at home through the stylised Sudanese architecture which appeared in the interwar colonial exhibitions, the Sub-Saharan colonies compelled French political attention as never before shortly after World War II and in face of severe colonial unrest elsewhere.

NEW DEVELOPMENTS

One of the most popular American magazines, *U.S. News and World Report*, published an article in its 30 April 1954 issue which referred to Dakar as 'Paris in Africa'.[4] An exaggerated and unfair comparison, the assertion nonetheless attests to the rapid growth of this city and, indirectly, to the economic investment that France was now making in this part of the world. The new economic development in France which consisted of state planning and financing of wartime recovery and modernisation was given an African counterpart with the establishment of FIDES, a well-chosen acronym that compressed the long title 'The Fund for Investment and Social and Economic Development of the Overseas Territories' (*Fonds d'Investissement et de Développement Economique et Sociale des Territoires d'Outre-Mer*). Established on 30 April 1946, this plan for economic development funnelled most of its money into 'infrastructure':

improvement of ports and railroads, construction of new airports and roads. Yet a considerable sum also went into education and health care, a somewhat higher proportion going to Equatorial Africa where such services were still rudimentary. Concurrently, private investors appeared on the scene, some seeing the financial handwriting on the wall in Indochina, therefore turning to what they perceived to be a more secure place; and others, caught up in the notion of a new economic community comprised of Europe and Africa – called 'Eurafrica' – seeing the opportunity for new trade patterns.

Soon a considerable number of Africans became plastic sandal-shod and began carrying the leather briefcase in which the French-man traditionally inserts his papers and his lunch. The bureau-cratisation of services grew along with the technical personnel who appeared from France, a condition that later led President Senghor to comment that Senegal could do with some 10 000 fewer bureaucrats. The rather dramatic incorporation of numbers of Africans into the European-based economy was enhanced in 1952 by the passage of the 'Lamine Guèye Law' which equalised employ-ment opportunities and salaries and wages among Europeans and Africans.

The French African cityscape changed dramatically. High-rise buildings appeared in Dakar and Abidjan, the capital of the Ivory Coast. *Rond-points*, the traditional French method for circulating traffic, also appeared in these places. And as automobiles raced through the growing coastal cities, a rural population entered them by other means of transportation, not employment, and thus created major housing problems. By 1948 Dakar had a population of 228 000 of whom 17 000 were European. Urban planning suddenly became a serious colonial business and economic development was submitted to the drawing-board and calculator as well: the techni-cian replaced the colonial officer.

These seemingly smooth, modernising developments in French Africa were taking place far away, in mood and space, from the one political upheaval which greatly disturbed the French in their territories below the equator. The violence which occurred on Madagascar, the island off the east coast of Africa, began early and intensely. There, a nationalist movement quickly grew, influenced in its demands by events in Indochina. Initial indications were strongly given during the debates of the First Constituent Assembly, when Malagasy representatives had demanded self-government, a request peremptorily dismissed by the French. Then, a successful mass party, the MDRM (*Mouvement Démocratique de la Rénovation Malgache*, the Democratic Movement for the Renovation of Madagascar) amassed some 200 000 members by 1947 and prepared a major uprising on 29 March 1947, in protest against French rule. The French were able to contain and put down the revolt by that autumn, inflicting severe reprisals. Madagascar thereafter sullenly followed the political patterns of the other French possessions of Sub-Saharan Africa, where peaceful evolution was the norm. Yet the revolt remained another tragic reminder of the growing discontent with French colonialism, wherever it had been forcibly established and maintained.

THE NEW POLITICS

Modern French African politics were inaugurated in Paris, not in any colonial city, the proof perhaps being Blaise Diagne's tenure as Dakar's representative to the French Chamber of Deputies in the metropolitan capital. Until the postwar era, the few Africans who were politically significant gained that status in Paris. (It is worth recalling that no African was present at the Brazzaville Conference of 1944.) This was equally true in 1946 as Black Africans proceeded to France to participate in the deliberations of the Constituent Assembly. While proportionately grossly underrepresented, the 64 Black Africans at that convention assumed an influential role, joining in the Intergroup of Indigenous Deputies which had been formed under the leadership of Ferhat Abbas after the First Constituent Assembly.

As the Second Constituent Assembly sat, the aspirations of Black Africans for colonial reform had largely been denied.[5] The representatives from these colonial territories had enthusiastically endorsed the constitution designed by the First Constituent Assembly, and the African electorate voted strongly in favour of this constitution which, however, had been rejected by the metropolitan voters. This was the constitution that would have introduced universal suffrage, abolished the two-college system of colonial rule, and would have assured the assimilationist political ideal which the Africans supported at the time. Their objective had not been independence, but rather the full realisation of a French Union in which they would be equals.

In the new constitution, accepted by the French electorate, equality prevailed not at the level of the grassroots but only at the level of high principle. The preamble spoke of equal rights for all peoples in the French Union, but individual articles imposed the two-college system, disallowed universal suffrage by the establishment of degrees of citizenship and accordingly vitiated the establishment of purposeful local assemblies in which Africans could assume major political authority. Although they voted for the new constitution, the African representatives did so with little enthusiasm and with great concern about their political future which now seemed Paris-centred rather than locally based because of the new restrictive clauses on local African political activity. It was apparent that the colonial centre still held.

Of immediate concern to the African representatives who had participated in the now concluded Constituent Assembly was the nature of their own political future, particularly on what foundation or structure they might, should, stand for office. The French political leadership and older African politicians like Lamine Guèye wished the Africans to use the established French political parties with which they were currently affiliated and which, like the French Socialist Party already, might establish African sections. Senghor initially agreed with this appraisal, but Félix Houphouet-Boigny, a medical assistant from the Ivory Coast, who had already organised agricultural workers there into a powerful political base, thought that the possibility of a distinctive African political party should be discussed. He called for a preliminary conference on the matter, to be held in Bamako, French Sudan, in 1946. This conference was followed by another in Treichville, a suburb of Bamako, Ivory Coast, in 1947, at which time the RDA was initiated.

The *Rassemblement Démocratique Africain* (Democratic African Rally), the first African party in the French possessions, modelled its tactics on those of the French Communist Party, which gave it support. However, the Communist Party was not radical in colonial affairs and had indeed espoused the assimilationist approach, thus not differing publicly with the other French parties over African colonial policy. Even though appearing radical at the time, the new party, in accord with general political sentiment at the time, did not yet utter a word for independence.

What the African representatives wanted was the fulfillment of the ideals of the French Union. More particularly, they were concerned with the general political relationship their territories and France should establish. Two alternatives existed: the federation of France with the two colonial federations of West and Equatorial Africa or the federation of France with the individual colonies in those colonial federations. Senghor pursued the first option, thinking that Africans would thus have a stronger voice in politics because they would have a larger political base in French Union activities. Houphouet-Boigny, on the contrary, wished political activity to be defined by the individual colony, a decision that in some measure resulted from his concern with preserving the wealth of the Ivory Coast, which he feared, were the French West African Federation retained as a unit, would be used to support financially weak areas such as Senegal.

This division of opinion became acute with the passing of the *Loi Cadre* or 'Enabling Act' of 1957 which constitutionally reformed the African colonies without the need for constitutional amendment. The law, pushed through by the Minister of Colonies Gaston Defferre, mayor of Marseilles, a city with strong economic ties to the Ivory Coast, and supported by Houphouet-Boigny, then a cabinet minister in the French government, both liberalised and decentralised the colonial administration. The law introduced universal suffrage, abolished the two college system, extended the power and responsibilities of the territorial assemblies and provided each with a council of ministers which, in effect, formed something of a shadow cabinet. The law did, however, make the governor of each territory president of the territorial council of ministers and did reserve to him major powers in matters of public order and finances. Thus sovereignty effectively remained in French hands.

The law was greeted much less enthusiastically by the African politicians. Senghor, with historical allusion clear in mind, referred to the *Loi Cadre* as the device which would allow the 'Balkanization of Africa'. Emphasizing the colonies rather than the federations, the law would allow the French to manipulate and manoeuvre, he forewarned. Other politicians objected to the law as being 'too little too late', with the promised political equality unrealised because of the powers reserved to the governors.

Whether the colonial federations could have been converted into meaningful African political units, as Senghor had hoped, is doubtful.

The federal principle worked nowhere for any length of time in any of the decolonised regions of the world, and these vast colonial administrative conveniences in French controlled Africa hardly responded to local topography, ethnicity or tradition. However, the French lack of interest in such a federal arrangement was suspect, seen by many as an indication of the government's desire to negotiate with individual colonies and thus continue to enjoy the advantages of a favourable balance of power – in short, to 'balkanize'.

All told, the *Loi Cadre* was a major piece of legislation, proclaimed by some as the most significant passed by the Fourth Republic. The law was a belated acknowledgement of the inadequacy and anachronism of the colonial provisions in the Constitution of the Fourth Republic. It was, furthermore, the means by which to prepare the African colonies for self-government, if not independence, and thus must be boldly figured into any consideration of the devolution of colonial authority.

In any event, by the time the law was passed, the political mosaic of African politics was quite well-established. Territorial political parties were in existence in each of the colonies and were intent on winning over local populations to their purpose which still remained greater autonomy, not independence.[6]

Local political affairs were also affected by regional ones. The change in the neighbouring British colonies in West Africa was not without effect. The Gold Coast, which became Ghana in 1957, was the first Black African colony to become independent, and its powerful leader, Kwame Nkrumah, espoused a Pan-Africanism that was appealing to Senghor, among others. One of the first state visits made by Nkrumah was to Sékou Touré in Guinea.

Equally significant was the changed status of Togo, a mandated territory from World War I and then a Trust territory from World War II. As the British proceeded to devolve their political authority in the portion of Togo over which they had jurisdiction, the French responded, giving their portion of Togo its autonomy in 1956, just before Ghana's independence, and its freedom in 1960.

DE GAULLE AND THE END OF SUB-SAHARAN AFRICAN EMPIRE

Such were the conditions that proceeded the advent of Charles de Gaulle to power again in 1958 and his resumption of a role in Black

African politics that he had not played since the Brazzaville Conference. One thing is certain: de Gaulle's range of options was now very limited. Within one year, between 1956 and 1957, the word 'independence' had entered the Black African political vocabulary, not as an imperative but as a possibility. Some student groups had already issued the demand, as had the Guinean trade union over which Sékou Touré held sway. Black Africans had spoken out in favour of Algerian independence, but the RDA Conference in Bamako had declared independence a 'right', not a necessity.

Some of the hesitancy of the new African leaders to seek independence came from their realisation of the economic difficulties that freedom might imply. Each of the territories had become very heavily dependent on France for financial and technological support as the FIDES plan became an important part of their finances and technical organisation. As individual states, none, save the Ivory Coast, would be economically self-sufficient.

In this rather confused, if not turbulent, political atmosphere, General de Gaulle, as new head of state, acted quickly and decisively. One part of the constitutional reforms he introduced was the structural alteration of the remnants of the old empire. He now called for a 'Community' which would replace the moribund French Union.

The new 'Community' was structured as a super-parliamentary government, with the president of the Republic also designated president of the Community, with a council of ministers presided over by the French premier, with a senate, and a court of arbitration. Heir to the French Union, more liberal and flexible in disposition than its predecessor, the Community proceeded from the old revolutionary ideal, as its forms were to be based 'on the common ideal of liberty, equality, and fraternity, and are designed to permit of democratic evolution ...'.[7]

There is no need to discuss the structure of the Community more fully because it was never realised, independence quickly superceding it. However, de Gaulle had allowed the overseas territories four options at the time the Constitution of the Fifth Republic was submitted to referendum. They were: assimilation (becoming departments of France), retention of their status as overseas territories in accordance with the *Loi Cadre* of 1956, election to become 'member states' of the Community with the future possibility of independence and immediate independence by a vote of 'no' to the referendum – the last option proposed when de Gaulle made a tour of Sub-Saharan Africa just before the referendum. Guinea chose the last option; the other territories chose to become member states. However, by 1960 all of them had emerged as independent, sovereign nations.

The Community was the last expression of *Plus Grande France*; the Community was, a hasty improvisation to bring what remained of nineteenth-century empire into accordance with late twentieth-century political desires and demands.

AFRICAN INDEPENDENCE

The Community fell apart before it was even set in place. Within two years, all of the African states had become independent, the result of little coordination, insufficient interest in pursuing common goals. If there was a catalyst that caused the experiment to explode quickly, it was Sékou Touré who had the audacity to vote 'no' to de Gaulle's referendum and then to incur the quick and fulsome wrath of the president who also had been a general. France immediately cut off all aid to Guinea and proceeded to remove its assets, even having the telephones ripped from the walls in an act of spite. De Gaulle's action was double-charged, personal anger and political concern, the latter the fear that if Guinea were not reprimanded and punished economically, the new member states of the new Community would also seek independence as no advantage would be found in further participation in the organisation. However, with the aid of the Soviet Union and the praise of other African countries, Sékou Touré not only survived but even assumed a jaunty attitude of success.

What he had done beside tweak General de Gaulle's prominent nose was undermine the principle of federation dear to Senghor. The feared Balkanisation had erupted from within. Now, in an effort to save what was left, Senghor moved to join Senegal, Sudan, Dahomey and Upper Volta into the Mali Federation. However, only Sudan voted to support the venture, and the much restricted Mali Federation was further disadvantaged when de Gaulle refused to recognise it.

De Gaulle's position was obvious, assumed as it was long before this particular development. An astute politician, he realised that the federations might be strong enough to ask for independence, thus to dismember the Community. However, the difficulties now confronting the Community occurred in the political gulf existing between Senghor and Houphouet-Boigny, the former chiefly interested in a confederation rather on the lines of the British Commonwealth, the latter interested in a federation much like what the French Union proposed – and what de Gaulle had hoped the new Community might be.

Into that extensive political gulf the Community fell, and there it sank.

Senghor now asked for independence for the Mali Federation under the constitutional provisions of the Community and de Gaulle, in a belated effort to save what he might, granted it. Houphouet-Boigny, irritated by this action, acted unilaterally, announcing that the four member states of his *Conseil d'Entente*, an effort he had undertaken to achieve economic cooperation among Upper Volta, Dahomey, Niger and the Ivory Coast, would simply declare their independence and seek Community approval afterward.

And so he and so they did. And so the French Community disappeared. If there is irony in this historical matter, it was this: those who were most interested in constructing something durable of the Franco-African political relationship, de Gaulle, Senghor and Houphouet-Boigny, were all responsible to some considerable degree for its very rapid, and therefore almost unnoticed disappearance from the world scene.

Yet the Community's short political life provided a moment of needed transition, one in which the African colonies adapted French institutions in order to become independent states. Primarily modelling themselves on the Fifth Republic, with a strong head of state, these new nations all completed constitutions in a short period of time, between the months of January and March 1959. The new states were thus supporting what François Tombolalbaye, soon to be President of the Republic of Chad, described in a now famous declaration of 1 July 1959, as 'our profound belief in the principles of a democracy that France has taught us . . .'.

Conclusion

On the waterfront of Marseille, there stands a small triumphal arch, erected in the interwar period to those who had formed the colonial empire and who had sacrificed their lives for it. This piece of masonry is of no consequence today. It opens on to a sea that no longer carries the freight of empire, and it is located nowhere near a major airport from which the French as tourists depart to places that appear as exotic in our age of instantaneous communications as they did when the force of empire was carried forward in steel hulls and projected by artillery shells.

Of entirely different shape from that turn-of-the-century world which was simply divided between mother country and colony, or the 'West' and the 'rest of the world', today's global society is constructed on lines of organisation which make overseas empire seem, in retrospect, a poorly arranged structure, an inefficient way of doing things. Multi-national corporations, like so many of the computer and television manufacturers; 'off-shore' manufacture, like the Japanese automobile plants in the United States; 'mini' industrial states, like Hong Kong and Taiwan; and international consortia, like the ones producing rockets and aircraft in Europe – all define an age in which colonial politics and colonial economics appear to be far-recessed in the past, not just removed by a few decades.

Furthermore, the geographical configurations of power have been reworked. Now the 'Pacific Rim', where France never played a significant role, is the magic circle of world economics and technological progress. 'An immense Asia standing beside a miniscule Europe', was the description given it already in 1936 by one critic.[1] However, Europe itself is not at this moment miniscule or sharply divided into contending political states. The French of today need not assume the attitude of their predecessors and look fretfully at the 'Blue Line of the Vosges'. France's European future is one shared with a united Germany and found in a new and vast economic community which will eventually form one large marketplace, anticipated to be the largest in the world. In such vast structures the old political and economic justifications for imperialism ring no more and, if they did, they would only ring hollow.

CRITICAL APPRAISALS OF DECOLONISATION AND NEO-COLONIALISM

First popularised by the French, although first introduced in English in the 1920s, 'decolonization' became an ideologically freighted term as much as an incisively analytical one. From the French perspective, the term implied the formal renunciation of political domination, symbolically expressed by the lowering of the flag. From the perspective of the formerly colonised peoples, the term was far more complicated, far more nuanced.

To decolonise was to cleanse as well as to reject. Almost all authors writing of the situation in the French possession in which they had resided saw the withdrawal of the French as the opportunity for cultural renewal, for the creation of a new sort of community, one distinguished by solidarity, cooperation and unity, one in which Western competitive individualism and class distinctions would not exist. Frantz Fanon, in his *Wretched of the Earth*, stated that decolonisation unified the formerly colonised people '. . . by the radical decision to remove from it its heterogeneity, and by unifying it on a national, sometimes a racial basis'.[2]

In Sub-Saharan Africa, decolonisation was seen to offer the opportunity for the creation of a new society mollified by traditional African values, a humanistic symbiosis. Léopold Sédar Senghor gave a lecture at Oxford University in 1961 in which he explained his rejection of capitalism because it was spiritually alienating and called for an African Socialism which would affirm a traditional *'community-based society'* (the italics his) that would be directed to the problem of keeping 'the fervor of the black soul alive . . .'.[3] Sékou Touré, then the radical president of Guinea, in 1961 coined the adjective 'communaucratic', which he stated expressed 'the collective society and social solidarity' of and assured an enviable humanistic foundation for his nation.[4]

Along with notions of spiritual renewal went expressions of concern over the unwanted durability of institutional structures and established patterns of economic behaviour. Even as FIDES, the economic development plan for Africa was in operation, its benefits to the French were as great as to the Africans to whom it was directed, because French banks, French shipping lines and French products all figured into the projects undertaken, the profits of these activities benefiting France and certain Frenchmen more than Africa and Africans, it was contended. The alteration of earlier colonial patterns of trade in the days of political devolution is nowhere better evidenced than in the growth of the bauxite industry in Guinea. There, after World War II, French and Americans engaged in extensive mining to obtain the raw material from which the resultant aluminium was primarily manufactured in the United States for products that benefited French households and served the aircraft industry as basic material. The value to Guinea was marginal, critics complained.[5]

Already in 1954, Jacques Berque, a French university professor and a North African by birth, argued that independence had brought a change of direction: economic development encouraged by the new state, not imposed as it had been in the former colony. The collusion – for so it was perceived by many critics – of the new nation state with the old colonial powers – and the United States – in the furtherance of corporate capitalism led to continuing 'dispossession'.[6]

This international economic network that proved the formal colonial structure was, at the very least, obsolete was to be the primary element of criticism in the theory of 'neo-colonialism'.

Neo-colonialism was a cry of despair and a shout of complaint about the continuing inequities in a world that had been bifurcated by modern imperialism. The older terms 'haves' and 'have nots', popular in the interwar period, expressed the perceived distinction in a brutally clear manner. But now, the social science terminology of the university yielded 'developing nation' and, more gently, 'less developed nation'. The nicely graphed, upwardly-inclined line which represented the eighteenth and nineteenth-century doctrine of progress remained but was renamed 'modernization'.

IMPERIALISM AND MODERNISATION

Briefly effected at the time when the world order was changing from a rural-agrarian to an urban-industrial one, imperialism was less a modernising than a temporising force, a crude series of attempts to reconcile old and new, to assert the form of power traditionally maintained by the sword just when power was being produced by the generator, to rule by fiat when the time called for a show of hands.

Robert Delavignette, as sensitive and as forward-looking a colonial administrator as was ever found, rhapsodically revealed one element in this conjunction of old and new, that of nostalgia for the arcadian in an age of economic development. In the introductory chapter of his *Afrique Occidentale française* he wrote: 'The African residence that I left a few months ago seemed the place of a gentleman farmer', even though not far away there was the sight of factory smoke and the sound of truck traffic. The colonial mission had been this modernisation, Delavignette admitted, but 'there is also something else, and it is the land'.[7]

Such ambivalence, this fluctuation between official intentions and personal sentiments, between assuming the role of agent of modernisation and longing for the condition of country squire, is frequently noted in the literature produced by those French who were colonial administrators. Of course, the analogue of such mixed sentiments was the African one, the celebration of the land and of tradition that was found in the literature of *négritude*. The French and the Africans, if from a different angle of vision, sensed and were disturbed by the tension caused and the effects generated by modernisation.

However, the literature that was written on the subject was more intense than the activities that took place. Whether more might have been done to modernise the colonial empire in an age when the regulatory, not the interventionist state existed, when double-entry bookkeeping, not long-range planning, was the mode of procedure, is an interesting question, but one irrelevant to the fact that French domination was not so deep-rooted in most colonial territories, was not so structurally fixed, that it was not rather easily removed and with little lasting monuments or desires.

Nevertheless, modern imperialism was a modernising force, at least introducing the means of change at a time when the capitalist economy was widely expanding. Certainly the most ardent of imperialists claimed that imperialism was an economic necessity. Jules Ferry in his famous metaphor referred to imperialism as the safety valve on the industrial steam engine, the means by which to release pent-up economic force. Long before its critics denounced it as a crude capitalist enterprise and long before scholars carefully examined global economic behaviour, the imperialists devised balance sheets of empire in an effort both to persuade government and to entice private investors of its worth.

One way or the other, goes a popular academic argument, a world capitalist system would have emerged.[8] Imperialism was but its particular vehicle, not its cause or source. Today as one observes the radical changes currently affecting the last of the modern empires, that of the Soviet Union, the argument seems particularly acute. Economics, not politics, has been the apparent determinant of the current cultural shape of the globe.

THE EFFECTS OF FRENCH COLONIAL EMPIRE

Dismissing such considerations as highly conceptual, even ahistorical, the contemporary critic may turn away from such arguments to attend the particularities and peculiarities of French imperialism. In the long run, measured on the grand time scale that the French historian Ferdinand Braudel has called the *longue durée*, French imperialism may indeed prove to be inconsequential, a moment of glory followed by several moments of anguish, a brief span of time during which France was somewhat distracted from its continental concentration.

The effects of French imperialism may therefore be few. Certainly, those persons most directly involved with it, the administrators, were seldom trained to be other than 'bush' officers: keepers of the peace, collectors of the tax, roamers of the countryside. Their presence, not their programme, was what counted. They generally played their role as chief, as Robert Delavignette had described it. Among the main ironies of French imperialism is this one: the best trained colonial officials were those who appeared overseas after World War II, technicians and specialists who did not wear *casques coloniales* but undertook careful field studies, hovered over charts and blueprints, prepared schemes for economic development and urban planning.

Yet even when such recent developments are considered, can one determine whether colonial administration did anything more than regularly maintain a light touch and occasionally use a heavy hand? This question has been much debated, but in French no more incisively than by Jacques Berque. Berque concluded that modern imperialism was a surface matter, that it moved horizontally over the globe and across the cultures it encountered. 'Its superficial triumphs, which are evoked by the term "occupation", cover the complexity of the affair as well as the shallowness of its effects', he asserted.[9]

This argument is consonant with others which cast doubt on the assertion that imperialism and colonial rule had profound effect. Perhaps in economic, even social terms, they did not. Only in the major cities, particularly in the port cities, did the 'French way of things' prevail. Yet even there, the results were of a hybrid sort, visible in the familiar sight of a rubber-tired, horse-drawn cart or, more recently, the plastic container carried to the village water pump – or even discernible in that remarkable moment when the University of Dakar had on its faculty one of France's finest medieval scholars.

Yet, in the immediate, in the decades after decolonisation, the French colonial influence has remained strong. The French language continues to be a *lingua franca*, with major African authors writing in French. The French bureaucratic and judicial systems suffered no severe alterations. The constitutions that were quickly adapted in Sub-Saharan Africa were essentially French documents. And, with few exceptions, the old colonial regions re-established close relationships with France as they became nations. Léopold Sédar Senghor's famous line 'to assimilate, not to be assimiliated' seems to be a good summary phrase of these developments.

In a now frequently cited speech that he made to the International African Association meeting in Brussels in 1963, and given the beguiling title, '*Et maintentant, Lord Lugard?*', ('What now, Lord Lugard?'), the former French colonial administrator and historian, Hubert Deschamps, attempted an assessment of the relative success of the English and the French as colonial administrators in Africa. He concluded that the score in this colonial game was the same for each of the major colonising nations: 'One to one, Lugard. Match void'.[10] According to Deschamps, the English had won in their acceptance of African autonomy, but had lost in their system of 'indirect rule' because they had wished to maintain indigenous institutions. The French had lost on political assimilation but had won with their universalist approach, the assumption that all peoples were moving forward together and, therefore, that change of customary behaviour and evolution of existing institutions should be encouraged. Deschamps' contention was not different from Senghor's except in one particular: the source of the initiative. And therein lay the fundamental weakness, the overwhelming arrogance of modern imperialism: the assertion that the European knew best.

THE COLONIAL COHORT GROUP

The French officials who wished to maintain some semblance of empire and the colonial leaders who dissented from empire learned together, shared, if from different sides, a common experience. Thus, they formed something of a cohort group, became at worse what Germaine Tillion called 'complementary enemies', bound together and in opposition by the travail of decolonisation. They were, almost every one, of one generation. Awakened to concern by the battlefield sounds of World War I, questioning their own and their country's or their culture's place in the postwar world, they were young in fact and in thought, newly-arrived colonial administrators like Delavignette in Africa, newly-arrived students like Senghor in France.

The overarching figures, the two bigger-than-life because they lived so intensely and maintained such a clear, unchanging vision of things, were Ho Chi Minh and Charles de Gaulle, each successful in achieving the national redemption of his country.

This colonial cohort group, of whom Ho and de Gaulle were both unconscious leaders, was primarily united by the experiences of the two world wars and the dramatic changes that those wars wrought in empire. At the outset fundamentally unyielding, even though alert to their weakened position in the world, the French encountered the young in the colonial regions who were still uncertain of what the future might hold, but who were aware of the possibility of modification of the colonial situation. Most of these personalities underwent a political transformation not dissimilar to that of Ferhat Abbas. In his famous statement of 1936, Abbas said that he had vainly looked for an Algerian nation and could not find one; his future was therefore allied with that of France. But he shifted, as did the fate of France, during World War II, and by 1943, in his *Algerian Manifesto*, he was demanding recognition of Algeria as a nation.

This rather remarkable experience whereby one generation of leadership moved from support of French dominion, to requests for reform, to demands for independence and then to leadership of the new nations that emerged from the old colonies is most unusual, almost without precedent. Now that generation and that cohort group are nearly all gone from the seats of power, Houphouet-Boigny, the last one retaining a seat of power since the aged and feeble Habib Bourguiba, one time 'President for Life', was gently deposed in 1988.

The effects of that common experience and the respect, which was in some measure engendered by it on both sides, were most poignantly displayed on the occasion of Charles de Gaulle's death, when most of the new heads of state in former French Sub-Saharan Africa came to France to pay respect to the dead leader. There they stood, heads bowed, eyes tearful, as they looked at the newly turned grave at Colombey-les-Deux-Eglises.

THE FRENCH ATTITUDE AND THE COLONIAL REACTION TO EMPIRE

Those French who marked the departure of de Gaulle with sadness did not do so for colonial reasons but out of respect for the general-president's achievements in France and Europe. Never quite certain as to why they acquired the enterprise, whenever they bothered to think about it historically, the large majority of French were vastly disinterested in their vast empire. For all their efforts, the 'colonial party', a group of parliamentarians, publicists and a few businessmen, most active in the decade before World War I, could not interest the nation at large in the colonial cause. Launching a large number of organisations and publications – ranging from the French Society for the Emigration of Women to the Colonial Society of Fine Arts – they all sought an objective similar to that described by the Dupleix Committee in its manifesto of 1899: 'to attract attention to the colonies, to make them better understood, and to prepare those French capable of becoming colonists for the colonial life'.

Such widespread attention was never received. There were brief moments, special occasions when the world overseas directly entered the Frenchman's thought. Along with the major expositions in the interwar period, there were expeditions, such as the ones that the great automobile manufacturer André Citröen sponsored to Central Africa in 1926 and across Asia in 1931. A few literary efforts also brought empire home to parlour and bedroom. And so, in an indirect way, did the two French children's classics which are situated in the colonial environment. The first, which has already been mentioned, is Antoine de Saint Exupéry's *Le Petit Prince*. The other, which is the creation of Jean and Laurent de Brunhoff, who lived but a few kilometres from Paris, is *Barbar*, which, like Saint Exupéry's work, appeared in the interwar period. Recently, *Barbar* has been critically interpreted as a fable supporting colonialism by Ariel Dorfman in his *The Empire's Old Clothes* (1983).[11] Therein, the upright, fashionably attired and crowned Barbar is analysed as a thinly disguised symbol of what the *mission civilisatrice* and the policy of assimilation were all about. Barbar is, in Dorfman's reading, a representative of the colonised personality who has been made over, civilised, and then returned to the jungle as exponent of the mode of thinking and the habits he has aquired, along with a flashy motorcar.

Alongside the various *Barbar* books to be found at Parisian booksellers will be seen a different sort of volume, one of the many critical analyses of a development unexpected by the imperialists, immigration into France. One of the most serious disruptions of colonial empire in its terminal decade was the demographic movement. As the Algerian War concluded, French settlers in vast numbers – hundreds of thousands – left to relocate in a France that they did not know. They followed the tens of thousands of settlers who had been repatriated from Morocco and Tunisia. These, in turn, followed the many thousands of Algerians who had already migrated to France in search of work and who had become an alien proletariat engaged in low-paying service activities like refuse collection and street repair. They also were the workers most responsible for laying down the new track system on which the TGV (the rapid French electric trains) move between Paris and Marseille. Following this influx of Algerians and the many workers who came from Sub-Saharan Africa, an invidious racism arose with many outbursts of violence in sections of Paris and Marseille.

As France was confronted with this major problem, its former colonies sought to adjust to their place as modern nation states. The transition, which created tension between the old and the new and which implied a new collective 'personality', to use a term favoured at the time, was not only a subject of political debate but also of literary examination.

Among the many works which have been concerned with this question of cultural identity, two merit particular attention. Camara Laye personalises the condition in his autobiographical novel *The Dark Child* (1954), descriptive of a young man growing up in French Guinea in the last years of colonialism. 'Sometimes only the spirit of a tradition survives', Laye wrote, 'sometimes only its form.'[12] Yet the new may appear formless, difficult to measure, to adjust to individual purpose or use. Ousmane Sembène, the Senegalese author and film director, made that problem the basic situation of his well-received film, *The Mandat* (*Mandabi*), released in 1968. The elderly Ibrahama Deng, the central figure of the film, receives a money order from France which he may only redeem upon presentation of proper identification. In his futile quest to prove himself and thus lay hands on this unexpected gift, Ibrahama becomes anonymous, a 'one-dimensional man', when he is required to move outside of the Senegalese culture in which he was an identifiable personality into the 'modern', with its identity cards, ledgers and fixed administrative procedures. Humourous and poignant, the film is an artistic expression of Emile Durkheim's concept of *anomie* and a telling commentary on the modern bureaucracy imported from colonial France only to be imposed coldly on a more personalised African society where word of mouth rather than printed form was the preferred mode of expression.

This particular variant of the literature of social realism was familiar in the emerging novels and films produced in many of the regions undergoing political and economic transformation from colonial dependencies to sovereign states. That transitional condition is now also part of the historical past. Like the Fifth Republic in France, the new republics in the former colonial empire have acquired stability and direction. They have become states and societies not concerned with the memories or effects of a once Eurocentric world, but contending with the present problems of a global age in which many flags fly.

Notes

INTRODUCTION: THE FRENCH COLONIAL EMPIRE IN THE CONTEXT OF
MODERN HISTORY

1. L. Canard, Letter-reports in folder 13 G 309, *Archives de la
République du Sénégal*.
2. Raymond Aron, *France: Steadfast and Changing* (Cambridge, Mas-
sachusetts, 1960), p. 82.

1. HISTORICAL CONDITIONS

1. Jules Harmand, 'Les utilités coloniales et le point de vue français',
Questions diplomatiques et coloniales, 16 August 1910, p. 201 Also see n.à.,
'L'effort coloniale', *Revue de Paris*, 15 September 1902, pp. 426–7
2. Quoted in Lotti H. Eisner, *Murnau* (Berkeley, 1973), p. 211.
3. J. L. Gheerbrandt, *Notre empire* (Paris, 1943), p. 4.
4. See the perceptive interpretation of Jacques Marseille, *Empire
colonial et capitalisme français* (Paris, 1984), notably p. 85, pp. 89–92.
5. Moll, *L'âme de colonial: Lettres du Lieutenant Colonel Moll* (Paris,
1912), p. 29.
6. Gaston Varenne, 'Le musée permanent des colonies', *Art et Décora-
tion*, July 1931, p 68. On the exposition and its public significance, see
Raoul Girardet, *L'idée colonial en France: 1841–1962*, (Paris, 1972),
Chapter 0.
7. Pierre Lyautey, *L'empire colonial français* (Paris, 1931), p. vii.
8. Albert Camus, *The Plague*, trans. Stuart Gilbert (New York, 1948),
p. 5.
9. André Gide, *Travels in the Congo*, trans. Dorothy Bussy (Berkeley,
1962), pp. 10 and 71.
10. Alfred Fouillée, *Psychologie du peuple français*, 6th edition (Paris,
1914), p. 178.
11. Arthur Girault, *Principes de colonisation et de législation coloniale*
(Paris, 1921), p. 71.
12. See Marseille, op. cit., Chapter 2.

2. AN EMPIRE PEACEFUL AND DISTURBED

1. This paragraph is primarily derived from the fine analysis of David
H. Marr, *Vietnamese Tradition on Trial, 1920–1945* (Berkeley, 1981).

2. Frantz Fanon, *Black Skin, White Masks*, trans. Charles Lam Markham (New York, 1967), p. 38.

3. Léon Damas, 'Houquet', in Léopold Sédar Senghor, ed., *Anthologie négro-africaine* (Paris, 1954), p. 16.

4. Lyautey, op. cit., p. 528.

5. Albert Sarraut, *La mise en valeur des colonies françaises* (Paris, 1923), p. 91.

6. On the trust idea see Duncan Hall, *Mandates, Dependencies and Trusteeship* (Washington, 1948); and Kenneth Robinson, *The Dilemmas of Trusteeship* (London, 1956).

7. Albert Saurraut, op. cit., p. 19.

8. Ibid., p. 91.

9. See Christopher M. Andrew and A. S. Kanya-Forstner, *The Climax of French Colonial Expansion* (Stanford, 1981).

10. André Beaufre, *Strategy for Tomorrow* (New York, 1974), p. 5.

11. Blum cited in Joel Colton, *Léon Blum: The Humanist in Politics* (New York, 1966), pp. 465–6.

12. On the general political development of the Left, see David Wohl, *French Communism in the Making, 1914–1924* (Stanford, 1966).

13. Reprinted in Maurice Thorez, *Une politique de grandeur français* (Paris, 1945), pp. 114–203.

14. Doriot quoted in Girardet, op. cit., p. 141.

15. Ferhat Abbas, *La nuit coloniale* (Paris, 1962), p. 128.

16. André Malraux, *The Temptation of the West*, trans. Robert Hollander (New York, 1961), p. 19.

17. Robert Delavignette, *Les paysans noirs* (Paris, 1946), p. 108.

18. Robert Delavignette, *Humanisme et commandement* (Paris, 1946), p. 242. On Delavignette, see William B. Cohen, *Robert Delavignette on the French Empire* (Chicago, 1977).

19. Quoted by Delavignette as found in Cohen, op. cit., p. 56.

20. Delavignette quoted in Cohen, op. cit., p. 33.

21. Carde quoted in Ralph A. Austen, 'Varieties of Trusteeship: African Territories under British and French Mandate, 1919–1939', in Prosser Gifford and Wm. Roger Louis, *France and Britain in Africa* (New Haven, 1971), p. 530.

22. Georges Hardy, *La politique coloniale et le partage de la terre aux XIXe et XXe siècles* (Paris, 1937), p. 465.

3. THE CHANGING SCENE IN THE COLONIAL WORLD

1. Quoted in Jean Lacouture, *Ho Chi Minh: A Political Biography* (New York, 1968), p. 30.

2. Quoted in ibid., p. 30.

3. Hardy, op. cit., p. 464.

4. For his own assessment of the development, see Habib Bourguiba, *La Tunisie et la France: Vingt-cinq ans de la lutte pour la coopération libre* (Paris, 1954).

5. 'Batouala and the Winning of the Goncourt Prize', *Living Age*, February 4, 1922, p. 309. The most accessible and effectively translated edition of the novel is that of Barbara Beck and Alexandre Mboukis, *Batouala* (Washington, 1972).

6. Loc. cit., p. 307.

7. On *négritude*, see René Depestre, *Bonjour et adieu à la négritude* (Paris, 1980); Thomas Melone, *De la négritude dans la littérature négro-africaine* (Paris, 1962); and Irving L. Markowitz, *Léopold Sédar Senghor and the Politics of Négritude* (New York, 1969).

8. Léopold Sédar Senghor, 'A New York', in Léopold Sédar Senghor, *Poèmes* (Paris, 1964), p. 117.

9. Aimé Césaire, *Return to My Native Land* (Paris, 1968), p. 101.

10. Ibid., p. 53.

11. On social and economic conditions in Indochina, see William J. Duiker, *The Rise of Nationalism in Vietnam, 1900–1941* (Ithaca, 1976); David G. Marr, *Vietnamese Anticolonialism, 1885–1925* (Berkeley, 1971); and Martin J. Murray, *The Development of Capitalism in Colonial Indochina (1870–1940)* (Berkeley, 1980).

12. See Charles Mangin, *La force noire* (Paris, 1909).

13. On Diagne and the issue of recruitment, see G. Wesley Johnson, *The Emergence of Black Politics in Senegal* (Stanford, 1971), notably pp. 183–95; and Marc Michel, 'La genèse du recrutement de 1918 en Afrique noire française', *Revue française d'histoire d'outre-mer*, 58: 433–50 (1977).

14. Nguyen Ai Qoc, *Le procès de la colonisation française* (Paris, n.d.), p. 10.

15. On Yen Bey, see Duiker, op. cit.

16. *Ho Chi Minh: Selected Writings, 1920–1969* (Hanoi, 1977), p. 37.

17. Abbas cited in Alf Andrew Heggoy, *Insurgency and Counter-Insurgency in Algeria* (Bloomington, 1972), p. 14.

18. Senghor formed part of an interesting group of authors who in 1943 wrote a supportive testimony to empire, a work only published at the end of World War II. Léopold Sédar Senghor, Robert Lemaignen and Prince Sisowath Youtevong, *La communauté impériale française* (Paris, 1945).

4. THE DESPAIR AND HOPE OF WAR

1. Charles de Gaulle, *L'appel* (Paris, 1954), p. 113.

2. Ibid., p. 128.

3. As Churchill wrote in his account of the event, 'To the world at large it seemed a glaring example of miscalculation, confusion, timidity and muddle. In the United States ... there was a storm of unfavourable criticism.', *Their Finest Hour* (Boston, 1949), p. 483.

4. De Gaulle, *L'unité* (Paris, 1956), p. 24.

5. Pierre Boisson cited in D. Bruce Marshall, *The French Colonial Myth and Constitution-Making in the Fifth Republic* (New Haven, 1973), p. 79.

6. On this subject see Robert O. Paxton, *Parades and Politics at Vichy* (Princeton, 1966).

7.   Franklin D. Roosevelt, Speech of 15 May 1941, in *The Public Papers and Addresses of Franklin D. Roosevelt* 1941 Volume (New York, 1950), p. 159.

8.   Statement of Anthony Eden to Winston Churchill quoted by Wm. Roger Louis, *Imperialism At Bay* (New York, 1978), p. 228.

9.   Cited in René Pinon, 'Après la chute de Porte-Arthur', *Revue des Deux Mondes*, 1 June 1905, p. 552.

10.   Hardy, op. cit., p. 314.

11.   See Winston Churchill, *The Hinge of Fate* (Boston, 1950), Chapter 2: "Decision for 'Torch'".

12.   De Gaulle, *L'unité*, p. 32.

13.   See de Gaulle, op. cit., 'Alger'; and Dorothy Shipley White, *Black Africa and De Gaulle: From the French Empire to Independence* (University Park, Pennsylvania, 1979).

14.   See David Lancaster, *The Emancipation of French Indochina* (London, 1961); and Ellen Hammer, *The Struggle for Indochina, 1940–1955* (Stanford, 1966).

15.   Elliott Roosevelt, *As He Saw It* (New York, 1946), p. 115.

16.   De Gaulle, *L'unité*, p. 125.

17.   On the conference and its effects, see Marshall, op. cit., 102–15.

18.   De Gaulle, *L'unité*, p. 225.

19.   The discourse is reprinted in its entirety in the documents following the text of *L'unité*, pp. 477–80.

20.   *La conférence africaine française, Brazzaville, 30 janvier 1944–8 février 1944* (Algiers, 1944), p. 35.

21.   Ralph Bunche quoted in Louis, op. cit., p. 45.

22.   Reprinted in John P. Halstead, *Rebirth of a Nation: The Origins and Rise of Moroccan Nationalism, 1912–1944* (Cambridge, Mass., 1967), p. 280.

23.   Reprinted in Abbas, op. cit., p. 141.

24.   Pleven quoted in Rudolph Albertini, *Decolonisation*, trans. Francisca Garvie (New York, 1971), p. 366.

25.   De Gaulle's chief insistence, however, was on the importance of the French colonial empire to France's postwar role as a great power. As he argued privately to President Roosevelt during his brief visit to Washington, 'How can she play that [role] if she is kept from global decisions, if she loses her African and Asian possessions [*prolongements*]...?', *L'unité*, p. 293.

5.   CAUTION AND CONFUSION

1.   Jean-Jacques Servan-Schreiber, *Lieutenant in Algeria*, trans. Ronald Matthews (New York, 1957), pp. 42–8.

2.   On Moutet's position see Marshall, op. cit., p. 254.

3.   *Major Addresses, Statements and Press Conferences of General Charles de Gaulle, May 19, 1958–January 31, 1964* (New York, 1964), pp. 114–17.

4.   De Gaulle, speech printed in *Le Monde* 31 December 1959, trans. and reprinted in Roy C. Macridis, *De Gaulle: Implacable Ally* (New York, 1966), p. 90.

5.   Delavignette in Robert Delavignette and Charles-André Julien, eds, *Les constructeurs de la France d'Outre-mer* (Paris, 1946), p. 47.
6.   Sisowath Youtevong quoted in Girardet, op. cit., p. 189.
7.   Stanley Hoffmann in Stanley Hoffmann *et al.*, *In Search of France* (New York, 1963), p. 15.
8.   Frequently quoted and from a celebrated speech given on 27 August 1946, this statement is found in Marshall, op. cit., p. 252. In addition to Marshall on the colonial empire and the constitutional arrangements of the Fourth Republic, see Gordon Wright, *The Reshaping of French Democracy*, (New York, 1948).
9.   Emile Tersen, *Histoire de la colonisation* (Paris, 1950), p. 127.
10.   See Marshall, op. cit., pp. 215–24.
11.   Quoted in ibid., p. 294; and in Wright, op. cit., p. 215.
12.   Cited in Bernard Fall, *The Two Viet-Nams* (2nd ed., London, 1967), p. 52.
13.   Cordell Hull, *The Memoirs of Cordell Hull*, Vol. II (New York, Macmillan, 1948), p. 1235.
14.   Sartre, 'Préface', Fanon, *The Wretched of the Earth*, trans. Constance Farrington (New York, 1966), p. 9.
15.   Fanon, op. cit., p. 33.
16.   Sartre, loc. cit., p. 11.

6.   DISSOLUTION

1.   On the French war in Indochina, see in particular the analyses of Bernard Fall. In addition to *The Two Viet-Nams*, there are *Street Without Joy* (New York, 1972) and *Vietnam Witness* (New York, 1966). Also see Edgar O'Ballance, *The Vietnamese War, 1945–54: A Study in Guerrilla Warfare* (London, 1964); Ellen Hammer, *The Struggle for Indochina, 1940–55*, (Stanford, 1966); and David Lancaster, *The Emancipation of French Indochina* (London, 1961).
2.   This development is clearly evaluated in George Herring, *America's Longest War: The United States and Vietnam, 1958–1975* (New York, 1979).
3.   Lucien Bodard, *The Quicksand War: Prelude to Vietnam* (New York, 1967), p. 3.
4.   On Ho see the biography of Jean Lacouture, *Ho Chi Minh: A Political Biography* (New York, 1968).
5.   Jacques Soustelle, 'Indochina and Korea: One Front', *Foreign Affairs* (October, 1950), p. 66.
6.   On the debacle of Dien Bien Phu, see Bernard B. Fall, *Hell in a Very Small Place: The Siege of Dien Bien Phu* (London: 1969); and the dramatic account of Jules Roy, *The Battle of Dienbienphu* (New York, 1963).
7.   See Melanie Billings-Yun, *Decision Against War: Eisenhower and Dien Bien Phu, 1954* (New York, 1988).
8.   *Ho Chi Minh: Selected Writings*, p. 171.

9. On the Geneva Conference, see James Cable, *The Geneva Conference of 1954 on Indochina* (Basingstoke, 1986); and Robert F. Randler, *Geneva 1954* (Princeton, 1969).

7. ACCUMULATING FAILURE: MOROCCO, TUNISIA AND ALGERIA

1. Interview entitled 'Algeria in Sight of Peace', *Réalités* (July 1956), p. 56.
2. For a critical interpretation, see Jacques Berque, *French North Africa: The Magrib Between Two World Wars* (New York, 1967).
3. On the history of the Suez incident, see Robert .R. Bowie, *Suez, 1956* (New York, 1964); and Wm. Roger Louis, *Suez* (New York, 1987).
4. N.a., *Morocco* (London, 1951), p. 117.
5. On general political developments in the country, see David Ling, *Tunisia: From Protectorate to Republic* (Bloomington, 1967); and Nora Salem, *Bourguiba and the Creation of Tunisia*, (Dover, N.H., 1984).
6. On France in Morocco, see John Halstead, *Rebirth of a Nation: The Origins and Rise of Moroccan Nationalism, 1832–44* (Cambridge, Mass., 1967); Douglas Ashford, *Political Change in Morocco* (Princeton, 1961); Simone Lacouture, *Le Maroc à l'épreuve* (Paris: 1968).
7. On the French colonial situation in Algeria, see Tony Smith, *The French Stake in Algeria, 1945–1962* (Ithaca, 1978); Vincent Confer, *France and Algeria: The Problems of Civil and Political Reform in Algeria, 1870–1930* (Syracuse, 1966); David Gordon, *The Passing of French Algeria* (London, 1966). A well-written book on the Algerians and their place in the French colonial scheme of things is Pierre Bourdieu, *The Algerians*, trans. Alan C. M. Ross (Boston, 1962).
8. Fanon, *The Wretched of the Earth*, p. 36, pp. 39–40.
9. On the Algerian politics of the Fourth and Fifth Republics, see Dorothy Pickles, *Algeria and France: From Colonialism to Cooperation* (New York, 1963).
10. Abbas, op. cit., p. 232.
11. On the Algerian War, see Alistair Horne, *A Savage War of Peace: Algeria, 1954–1962* (London, 1972); Michael T. Clark, *Algeria in Turmoil: A History of the Rebellion* (New York, 1959); and John E. Talbert, *War Without a Name: France in Algeria, 1954–1962* (New York, 1980).
12. This important development is analysed in Paul Clay Sorum, *Intellectuals and the Decolonization of France* (Chapel Hill, 1977), Chapter V: 'Terror in Algeria'.
13. Fanon, op. cit., p. 48.
14. This is the subject of the remarkable, prize-winning Italian film directed by Gillo Pontecorvo, *The Battle of Algiers*, 1967.
15. Germain Tillion, *France and Algeria: Complementary Enemies*, trans. Richard Howard (New York, 1961), pp. 4–5.
16. *Major Addresses … of General De Gaulle*, pp. 52–5.

8. THE PEACEFUL DEVOLUTION OF AUTHORITY: SUB-SAHARAN AFRICA

1.   Robert Delavignette, *Afrique occidentale française* (Paris, 1931), p. 5.

2.   On French colonial rule and its cultural impact in Africa, see Michael Crowder, *West Africa Under Colonial Rule* (Evanston, 1968) G. Wesley Johnson, ed., *Double Impact: France and Africa in the Age of Imperialism* (Westport, 1985); Prosser Gifford and Wm. Roger Louis, *France and Britain in Africa: Imperial Rivalry and Colonial Rule* (New Haven, 1971).

3.   Jean Paillard, *Periple noir* (Paris n.d.), pp. 39–40.

4.   'Paris in Africa', *U.S. News and World Report*, 20 April 1954, pp. 64–6.

5.   See Marshall, op. cit., pp. 208–316.

6.   On the movement toward nationalism and independence, see Ruth Schachter-Morgenthau, *Political Parties in French Speaking West Africa* (Oxford, 1964); Aristide P. Zolberg, *Creating Political Order: The One-Party States of West Africa* (Chicago, 1966); and Prosser Gifford and Wm. Roger Louis, eds, *The Transfer of Power in Africa* (New Haven, 1976).

7.   On the French Community, see Yves Guena, *Historique de la communauté* (Paris, 1962).

CONCLUSION

1.   Roger Labonne, *Le tapis vert* (Paris, 1936), p. 290.

2.   Fanon, *The Wretched of the Earth*, p. 37.

3.   Senghor, quoted in William H. Friedland and Carl G. Robserg, *African Socialism* (Stanford, 1967) p. 265.

4.   Quoted in ibid., p. 170.

5.   This argument is trenchantly made in Walter Rodney, *How Europe Underdeveloped Africa* (Washington, 1974), Chapter VI.

6.   Jacques Berque, *Dépossession du monde* (Paris, 1954), pp. 84–5.

7.   Delavignette, *Afrique occidentale française*, p. 5.

8.   Immanuel Wallerstein, *The Capitalist World-Economy* (Cambridge, 1979).

9.   Berque, op. cit., pp. 79–80.

10.   Hubert Deschamps, quoted in Robert O. Collins, ed., *Problems in the History of Colonial Africa 1860–1960* (Englewood Cliffs, 1970), p. 210.

11.   Ariel Dorfman, *The Empire's Old Clothes* (New York, 1983).

12.   Camara Laye, *The Dark Child* (New York, 1954), p. 64.

Select Bibliography

INTRODUCTORY NOTE

The brief bibliography that follows has been designed to complement the text with more detailed works of particular subjects. Such an arrangement is done with logic and out of necessity. As the reader will find, there are few books available in English – and not many more in French – that have treated either the history of modern French imperialism or its conclusion, decolonisation, in a broad or comprehensive manner. Indeed, with the exception of the British Empire, for which an impressive array of such overall studies does exist, modern imperialism and decolonisation as phenomena of global proportions have generally been treated in scholarly studies in one of three ways: comparatively, with the various national efforts juxtaposed and common themes or issues explored; topically, with particular issues – the rise of political parties, urbanisation, the role of the military – serving as the narrative theme; regionally, with the activities of the colonial power in a certain area – West Africa, Southeast Asia – analysed to determine the particular interaction of foreign rule and local culture.

Yet this said, the reader interested in studying one or more aspects of French decolonisation will be delighted to find an abundance of studies in English. Both the growing interest in 'regional' or 'area' studies after World War II and the new appeal of social science analysis concerned with constructs and comparisons – notably those of 'one party' states, 'charismatic leaders' and 'modernisation' – have encouraged a careful look backward, at the history anterior to these recent developments that have occurred and are still occurring in that vast 'Third World', which was marked by and then emerged from modern European imperialism.

GENERAL STUDIES

On French decolonisation in a global context:

RUDOLPH ALBERTINI, *Decolonisation: The Administration and the Future of the Colonies, 1919–1960*, trans. by Francisca Garvie (New York, 1971).
FRANZ ANSPRENGER, *The Dissolution of the Colonial Empires* (London, 1989).
RAYMOND F. BETTS, *Uncertain Dimensions: Western Overseas Empires in the Twentieth Century* (Minneapolis and London, 1985).
RUPERT EMERSON, *From Empire to Nation* (Cambridge, Mass., 1960).
HENRI GRIMAL, *Decolonisation: The British, French, Dutch and Belgian Empires* (London, 1978).
MILES KAHLER, *Decolonization in Britain and France* (Princeton, 1984).

On the French colonial empire and decolonisation;

CHRISTOPHER M. ANDREW and A. S. KANYA-FORSTNER, *The Climax of French Imperial Expansion, 1914–1924* (Stanford, 1981).
RAYMOND F. BETTS, *Tricouleur, A Brief History of the French Overseas Empire* (London, 1978).
HENRI BRUNSCHWIG, *French Colonialism, 1871–1914: Myths and Realities* (New York, 1968).
JAMES J. COOKE, *New French Imperialism, 1880–1910: The Third Republic and Colonial Expansion* (Hamden, Conn., 1973).
JEAN GANIAGE, *L'expansion coloniale de la France sous la Troisième République* (Paris, 1968).
A. S. KANYA-FORSTNER, *The Conquest of the Western Sudan: A Study in French Military Imperialism* (Cambridge, 1969).
PAUL CLAY SORUM, *Intellectuals and Decolonization in France* (Chapel Hill, 1977).
XAVIER YACONO, *Histoire de la décolonisation française* (Paris, 1969).

n theories, policies and practices:

RAYMOND F. BETTS, *Assimilation and Association in French Colonial Theory, 1890–1914* (New York, 1961).

WILLIAM B. COHEN, *Rulers of Empire: The French Colonial Service in Africa* (Stanford, 1971).

RAOUL GIRARDET, *L'idée coloniale en France, 1871–1962* (Paris, 1972).

MARTINE LOUTFI, *Littérature et colonialisme* (Paris, 1971).

D. BRUCE MARSHALL, *The French Colonial Myth and Constitution Making in the Fourth Republic* (New Haven, 1971).

JACQUES MARSEILLE, *Empire colonial et capitalisme français: Histoire d'un divorce* (Paris, 1984).

AGNES MURPHY, *The Ideology of French Imperialism* (Washington, 1948).

MARTIN J. MURRAY, *The Economic Development of Capitalism in Indochina (1870–1940)* (Berkeley, 1980).

On dissent from colonialism and protest against it:

FERHAT ABBAS, *Guerre et révolution d'Algérie: La nuit coloniale* (Paris, 1962).

JACQUES BERQUE, *Dépossession du monde*, (Paris, 1964).

AIMÉ CÉSAIRE, *Discourse on Colonialism*, trans. by Joan Pinkham (New York, 1972).

FRANZ FANON, *The Wretched of the Earth*, trans. by Constance Farrington (New York, 1966).

ALBERT MEMMI, *The Colonizer and the Colonized* (Boston, 1965).

NGUYEN-A-QUOC, *Le procès de la colonisation française* (Paris, n.d.).

LÉOPOLD SÉDAR SENGHOR, *African Socialism*, trans. by Mercer Cook (New York, 1959).

On Indochina and Vietnam:

MELANIE BILLINGS-YUN, *Decision Against War: Eisenhower and Dien Bien Phu, 1954* (New York, 1988).

BERNARD B. FALL, ed., *Ho Chi Minh on Revolution: Selected Writings, 1920–1966* (New York, 1967).
——, *Street Without Joy* (New York, 1972).
——, *The Two Viet-Nams, A Political and Military Analysis* (London, 1963).
WILLIAM J. DUIKER, *The Rise of Nationalism in Vietnam, 1900–1941* (Ithaca, 1976).
ELLEN HAMMER, *The Struggle for Indochina, 1940–1955* (Stanford, 1966).
GEORGE C. HERRING, *America's Longest War: The United States and Vietnam, 1950–1975* (New York, 1979).
JEAN LACOUTURE, *Ho Chi Minh: A Political Biography* (New York, 1968).
DAVID LANCASTER, *The Emancipation of French Indochina* (London, 1961).
DAVID G. MARR, *Vietnamese Anticolonialism, 1885–1925* (Berkeley, 1971).
——, *Vietnamese Tradition on Trial, 1920–1945* (Berkeley, 1981).
PUL MUS, *Viet-nam: sociologie d'une guerre* (Paris, 1952).
EDGAR O'BALLANCE, *The Indochina War. 1945–54. A Study in Guerrilla Warfare* (London, 1964).
MILTON E. OSBORNE, *The French Presence in Cochinchina and Cambodia: Rule and Response (1859–1905)* (Ithaca, 1969).
JULES ROY, *The Battle of Dienbienphu* (New York, 1963).

On North Africa:

DOUGLAS ASHFORD, *Political Change in Morocco* (Princeton, 1961).
JACQUES BERQUE, *French North Africa: The Maghrib Between Two World Wars* (New York, 1967).
MICHAEL T. CLARK, *Algeria in Turmoil: A History of the Rebellion* (New York, 1959).
VINCENT CONFER, *The Problem of Civil and Political Reform 1870–1920* (Syracuse, 1966).
DAVID GORDON, *The Passing of French Algeria* (London, 1966).
JOHN P. HALSTEAD, *Rebirth of a Nation: The Origins and Rise of Moroccan Nationalism, 1912–1944* (Cambridge, Mass., 1967).

ALF HEGGOY, *Insurgency and Counterinsurgency in Algeria* (Bloomington, 1972).

ALISTAIR HORNE, *A Savage War of Peace: Algeria, 1954–1962* (London, 1972).

SIMONE LACOUTURE, *Le Maroc à l'épreuve* (Paris, 1968).

DWIGHT L. LING, *Tunisia: From Protectorate to Republic* (Bloomington, 1967).

DOROTHY PICKLES, *Algeria and France: From Colonialism to Cooperation* (New York, 1963).

JEAN PONCET, *La Tunisie à la recherche de son avenir: indépendence ou néocolonialisme* (Paris, 1974).

TONY SMITH, *The French Stake in Algeria, 1945–1962* (Ithaca, 1978).

JOHN E. TALBERT, *War Without a Name: France in Algeria, 1954–1962* (New York, 1980).

I. WILLIAM ZARTMAN, *Morocco: Problems of New Power* (New York, 1964).

On Black Africa:

HENRI BRUNSCHWIG, *Noirs et blancs dans l'Afrique noire française* (Paris, 1983).

WILLIAM B. COHEN, *The French Encounter With Africans: White Response to Blacks, 1530–1880* (Bloomington, 1980).

G. WESLEY JOHNSON, ed., *Double Impact: France and Africa in the Age of Imperialism* (Westport, Connecticut, 1985).

PROSSER GIFFORD and WM. ROGER LOUIS, eds, *France and Britain in Africa; Imperial Rivalry and Colonial Rule* (New Haven, 1971).

——, *The Transfer of Power in Africa: Decolonization, 1940–1960* (New Haven, 1982).

JACQUES HYMANS, *Léopold Sédar Senghor: An Intellectual Biography* (Edinburgh, 1971).

JANHEINZ JAHN, *Neo-African Literature: A History of Black Writing* (New York, 1969).

C. WESLEY JOHNSON, *The Emergence of Black Politics in Senegal: The Struggle for Power in the Four Communes, 1900–1920* (Stanford, 1971).

LILLIAN KESTELOOT, *Les écrivains noirs de langue française. naissance d'une littérature* (Brussels, 1963).

IRVING L. MARKOWITZ, *Léopold Sédar Senghor and the Politics of Négritude* (New York, 1969).

RUTH SCHACHTER-MORGENTHAU, *Political Parties in French Speaking West Africa* (Oxford, 1964).

BRIAN WEINSTEIN, *Eboué* (New York, 1972).

DOROTHY S. WHITE, *Black Africa and de Gaulle: From the French Empire to Independence* (University Park, 1979).

ARISTIDE R. ZOLBERG, *Creating Political Order: The One Party-States of West Africa* (Chicago, 1966).

Index